Sarasota

Travel Guide

Discover and Explore the Cultural Coast of Florida:
Top Attractions and Things to Do

Lovelyn Hill

Table of Contents

Introduction

Welcome to Sarasota, Florida, a captivating destination that beckons with its natural beauty, cultural vibrancy, and endless possibilities for an unforgettable vacation. Nestled along the stunning Gulf Coast, Sarasota offers a unique blend of sun-soaked beaches, artistic delights, and a laid-back atmosphere that will leave you enchanted. As you embark on your journey to this hidden gem, let me introduce you to the wonders that await in the "Cultural Coast" of Florida.

Overview of Sarasota

Sarasota holds a special place in the hearts of those who have had the pleasure of experiencing its charms. Located on the southwestern coast of Florida, this city boasts miles of pristine, powdery white sandy beaches that stretch alongside the turquoise waters of the Gulf of Mexico. Siesta Key Beach, with its breathtaking beauty and tranquil ambiance, has rightfully earned global recognition as one of the world's best beaches.

Beyond the allure of its beaches, Sarasota's cultural scene is equally captivating. The city is renowned for its thriving arts community and has become a haven for artists, performers, and arts' enthusiasts. Immerse yourself in artistic wonders at the John and Mable Ringling Museum of Art, which houses an impressive collection of masterpieces, including works by European and American artists.

Music, dance, and theater take center stage in Sarasota, with the Sarasota Opera House and the Sarasota Ballet showcasing world-class performances throughout the year. The city's vibrant downtown area is a haven for art galleries, boutiques, and delightful eateries, where you can enjoy both local flavors and international cuisine.

Nature lovers and outdoor enthusiasts will find ample opportunities to explore the area's natural wonders. From kayaking through mangrove forests to hiking scenic trails in Myakka River State Park, there is no shortage of adventures in Sarasota. Embrace the spirit of the Gulf Coast as you embark on dolphin-spotting cruises, fishing charters, or simply basking in the sun on one of the many picturesque beaches.

Sarasota's rich history also adds to its beauty. Visit the Ca' d'Zan Mansion, the opulent former residence of John and Mable Ringling, and step into the world of the Roaring Twenties. Explore the Historic Spanish Point, where you can trace the city's heritage back to its Native American roots and discover the intriguing stories that shaped the area.

As you plan your visit to Sarasota, keep in mind that the city's subtropical climate ensures warm and inviting temperatures year-round. Whether you're seeking a winter escape or a summertime adventure, Sarasota offers a welcoming embrace in any season.

Why Visit Sarasota

Sarasota, Florida, beckons visitors from far and wide with its irresistible allure and an abundance of reasons to explore this captivating destination. Whether you're seeking relaxation, adventure, cultural indulgence, or simply a place to rejuvenate, Sarasota offers an enchanting escape like no other. Here, I unravel the many irresistible experiences that await you in the "Cultural Coast" of Florida.

Sun-Kissed Beaches: Sarasota is a paradise for sun-seekers and beach lovers. With its pristine coastline and glistening turquoise waters, the city boasts some of the most breathtaking beaches in the world. Siesta Key Beach, consistently ranked among the top beaches globally, entices you with its powdery white sands that feel as soft as silk beneath your toes. Whether you're basking in the sun, taking leisurely walks along the shore, or enjoying water sports like paddleboarding or kayaking, Sarasota's beaches provide the perfect setting for relaxation and rejuvenation.

Cultural Riches: Immerse yourself in the vibrant arts and cultural scene that Sarasota is renowned for. The city is home to the iconic John and Mable Ringling Museum of Art, a treasure trove of European, American, and Asian artworks. Explore the museum's vast collection, including stunning masterpieces by renowned artists. The Sarasota Opera House and the Sarasota Ballet present world-class performances, showcasing the incredible talent that graces Sarasota's stages. Dive into the local arts scene by visiting art galleries, attending art festivals, or experiencing live music performances that fill the air with melody and rhythm.

Natural Beauty: Sarasota boasts an abundance of natural wonders waiting to be discovered. Venture into Myakka River State Park, where you can traverse scenic trails, spot wildlife, and even embark on an adventurous airboat tour. Experience the serenity of the Marie Selby Botanical Gardens, where lush tropical plants and vibrant orchids delight the senses. For outdoor enthusiasts, Sarasota is a gateway to kayaking through peaceful mangrove tunnels, paddleboarding along scenic bays, and exploring nature preserves that showcase the area's biodiversity.

Delightful Dining: Sarasota's culinary scene is as diverse as its delicious taste. From waterfront seafood restaurants offering the freshest catch of the day to quaint cafes serving delectable pastries, the city promises culinary delights to satisfy every palate. Embrace the local flavors and indulge in regional specialties such as succulent Gulf shrimp, juicy Florida oranges, and mouthwatering Key lime pie. Sarasota's dining establishments offer a gastronomic journey that reflects the city's coastal and diverse influences.

Year-round Events: Sarasota is a city that celebrates life with a vibrant calendar of events throughout the year. Immerse yourself in the creative energy of the Sarasota Film Festival, showcasing a diverse selection of international films. Unleash your inner foodie at Sarasota Restaurant Week, where top local eateries offer special menus and exclusive culinary experiences. The Sarasota Chalk Festival transforms the streets into outdoor galleries, as renowned artists create stunning chalk art masterpieces. Beyond these, the city hosts art exhibitions, live performances, and cultural events that infuse every corner with excitement and inspiration.

Hospitality and Relaxation: Sarasota embraces you with warm hospitality, ensuring a seamless and enjoyable experience. The city offers a range of accommodation options to suit various preferences, from luxurious beachfront resorts to boutique hotels and cozy vacation rentals. Unwind by the pool, rejuvenate with spa treatments, or soak in the serene surroundings of your chosen haven. The friendly locals and laid-back atmosphere create an inviting ambiance that instantly makes you feel at home.

Geography

Nestled along the southwestern coast of Florida, Sarasota is blessed with a geography that blends coastal beauty, lush greenery, and a unique blend of urban and natural landscapes. As you embark on your journey to this captivating destination this year, let me guide you through the remarkable geography of Sarasota.

Coastal Charm: The highlight of Sarasota's geography is its stunning coastline that stretches for miles along the Gulf of Mexico. With its pristine, sandy beaches and crystal-clear azure waters, the coast is a haven for sun-lovers, water enthusiasts, and nature lovers alike. Siesta Key Beach, Lido Beach, and Crescent Beach are just a few of the renowned coastal gems that await your exploration. Whether you're seeking a peaceful retreat or thrilling water sports adventures, Sarasota's coast offers a diverse range of experiences to suit your taste.

Barrier Islands: Sarasota has a chain of beautiful barrier islands, each showcasing its unique character and natural wonders. Located just off the coast, these islands serve as a haven for wildlife, outdoor activities, and blissful relaxation. Siesta Key, Casey Key, and Longboat Key are among the most popular islands, offering pristine beaches, luxurious resorts, and a serene ambiance. These islands provide a tranquil escape for solace amidst nature's splendor.

Lush Landscapes: Beyond the coastline, Sarasota's geography boasts an abundance of lush greenery and natural landscapes. The city is home to stunning parks, nature preserves, and gardens that invite exploration and appreciation of Florida's rich biodiversity. Myakka River State Park, with its vast marshes, lakes, and wetlands, offers hiking, kayaking, and birdwatching opportunities. The Marie Selby Botanical Gardens showcases an exquisite collection of orchids and tropical plants, creating a tranquil oasis in the heart of the city. As you explore Sarasota's green spaces, be prepared to encounter towering palm trees, vibrant flowers, and the gentle melodies of native birds.

Inland Wonders: Sarasota's geography extends beyond its coastline and serene landscapes. The city is characterized by a mix of urban development, residential communities, and vibrant downtown areas. The downtown district is a hub of cultural activities, with its lively arts scene, boutique shops, and internationally inspired cuisine. The skyline is punctuated by modern architecture and historic buildings, creating a vibrant blend of old and new. As you navigate through the city, you'll discover charming neighborhoods, picturesque canals, and a sense of welcoming warmth from the local community.

Waterways and Bay: Sarasota is defined by its intricate network of waterways, including rivers, bays, and canals. The city is embraced by Sarasota Bay, a picturesque body of water connecting the mainland to the nearby islands. Here, you will relish the opportunity to explore the bay, whether on a leisurely cruise, fishing excursions, or navigating through its calm waters on a kayak or paddleboard. The bay also provides a stunning backdrop for waterfront dining and sunset strolls, creating unforgettable experiences.

Climate: Sarasota's geography is complemented by its pleasant subtropical climate, characterized by warm temperatures, abundant sunshine, and gentle Gulf breezes. The city enjoys mild winters, making it a sought-after destination to escape colder climates. Summers bring warmer temperatures, perfect for beachside relaxation and outdoor adventures. With its inviting climate, Sarasota offers a year-round destination where you can embrace outdoor activities and soak in the natural beauty of the region.

Climate

Sarasota, Florida, enjoys a delightful subtropical climate that embraces you with its warm temperatures, abundant sunshine, and gentle Gulf breezes. Throughout the year, Sarasota offers an inviting environment for outdoor activities, beachside relaxation, and exploration of its natural wonders.

Winter (December to February)

Sarasota's winter months are mild and pleasant, providing a welcome escape if you're seeking respite from colder climates. Daytime temperatures range from the low 70s to the mid-70s°F (21-24°C) and nights tend to be in the low 50s°F (10-12°C). While occasional cooler days and chilly evenings can occur, they are typically short-lived. Winter presents a perfect opportunity to soak up the warm sunshine on the beaches, explore the city's vibrant arts and cultural scene, and partake in various outdoor activities amidst comfortable temperatures.

Spring (March to May)

As spring emerges in Sarasota, temperatures gradually begin to rise, offering a transition from the mildness of winter to the warmer days ahead. Daytime temperatures hover between the high 70s to low 80s°F (25-28°C), and evenings remain pleasant in the mid-60s°F (18-20°C). Spring is a remarkable time to experience Sarasota's natural beauty as flowers bloom, wildlife thrives, and the city comes alive with a myriad of outdoor events and festivals. Whether you're strolling through gardens, exploring parks, or engaging in water activities, spring offers the perfect weather for exploration and rejuvenation.

Summer (June to August)

Sarasota's summer months bring warmer temperatures, delivering a paradise for sun-seekers and beach enthusiasts. Daytime temperatures soar into the high 80s to low 90s°F (31-33°C), and evenings remain comfortably warm in the mid-70s°F (24-26°C). Summer also brings increased rainfall, typically in the form of afternoon thunderstorms that pass quickly, leaving the air refreshed. The warm waters of the Gulf of Mexico invite you to dive into aquatic adventures, while the vibrant local culture provides an array of indoor and outdoor entertainment options to beat the heat.

Fall (September to November)

Autumn arrives in Sarasota with gradually cooling temperatures and a sense of tranquility in the air. Daytime temperatures range from the high 70s to low 80s°F (25-28°C), with evenings cooling down to the mid-60s°F (18-20°C). Fall is a delightful time to explore the city's parks and nature preserves as the foliage begins to change colors, presenting picturesque landscapes. With fewer crowds and pleasant weather, it's an ideal season for outdoor activities, dining al fresco, and discovering the rich cultural heritage of Sarasota.

Throughout the year, Sarasota benefits from its proximity to the Gulf Coast, which moderates temperatures and brings refreshing sea breezes. The city typically enjoys around 251 sunny days per year, making it a haven for a sun-kissed vacation. While Sarasota thrives under a subtropical climate, it is important to note that occasional hurricanes or tropical storms can occur, predominantly during the late summer and early fall months. It is advisable to stay informed about weather conditions and follow any safety advisories if they arise.

History of Sarasota

Pre-Colonial Era: The Native Foundations

Long before European settlers stepped foot on Florida's Gulf Coast, the area now known as Sarasota was inhabited by the Native American tribes, primarily the Calusa. The Calusa were known for their complex society and extensive shell mounds, some of which can still be seen today. They fished the abundant waters and navigated the lush mangrove forests that characterized the region. However, with the arrival of Spanish explorers in the 16th century, the Calusa population was devastated by disease and conflict, leading to their eventual disappearance by the late 1700s.

Spanish Exploration and Colonial Influence

The history of Sarasota as part of modern America began in 1513 when Spanish explorer Juan Ponce de León possibly sailed into Sarasota Bay, christened "Zarazote." Over the next few centuries, the area remained largely unsettled by Europeans but was noted in Spanish maps and logs. It wasn't until the 18th century that Spain, through missions and military outposts, attempted to establish more control over Florida, though these efforts were often disrupted by the local Seminole tribes and other factors.

The Pioneering Era: 1800s

In the early 19th century, after Florida became a U.S. territory following the Adams-Onís Treaty of 1819, American settlers began to show interest in Sarasota. The first significant settler was William Whitaker, who established a homestead around the Sarasota Bay area in the 1840s. The fertile land and abundant fishing quickly attracted more settlers. Sarasota was officially incorporated as a town in 1902, spurred by the extension of the railroad to the area, which linked it with larger markets and led to a population increase.

The 20th Century: Development and Transformation

The 20th century marked a period of rapid growth and transformation for Sarasota. In the early 1900s, influential figures such as Bertha Palmer, a wealthy socialite and businesswoman from Chicago, invested heavily in the region. She purchased thousands of acres for agriculture and cattle ranching, which drastically changed the economic landscape of Sarasota. Her influence also attracted other wealthy industrialists, who built luxurious homes and helped develop the area as a tourist destination.

The Sarasota School of Architecture

Post World War II era ushered in an architectural movement known as the Sarasota School of Architecture, which became a defining feature of the region. Pioneered by architects like Paul Rudolph and Victor Lundy, the movement embraced modernist ideas with a focus on subtropical climates. The structures characterized by this style featured large sunshades, innovative use of materials, and seamless indoor-outdoor spaces. This architectural innovation mirrored Sarasota's growing status as a cultural hub, with the establishment of numerous arts institutions, including the Sarasota Ballet and the Sarasota Opera.

Contemporary Sarasota: A Cultural Capital

Today, Sarasota is known as the cultural capital of Florida, boasting a vibrant arts scene that includes numerous theaters, galleries, and the acclaimed Ringling Museum of Art. The city's economy is supported by tourism, education, and health care. The legacy of the arts is maintained by institutions such as the Sarasota School of Art and Design and the annual Sarasota Film Festival, which draws visitors from all over the globe.

Therefore, prepare to embark on an unforgettable journey filled with sunny days, artistic marvels, lush landscapes, and warm Gulf breezes. Let Sarasota captivate you with its beauty, inspire you with its cultural treasures, and envelop you in its relaxed and welcoming ambiance. I invite you to dive into this Sarasota Travel Guide and discover all the wonders that await in this enchanting coastal paradise.

Chapter 1: Planning Your Trip

Best Time to Visit

Sarasota, Florida, is a mesmerizing destination that offers a multitude of experiences throughout the year. To ensure that you make the most of your visit to this vibrant coastal city, it is essential to consider the best time to plan your trip. With its subtropical climate, Sarasota boasts different seasons, each with its unique charm. Let me guide you through the optimal time frames to visit, so you can tailor your trip to suit your preferences and interests.

Winter (December to February)

If you yearn for a respite from colder climates and dream of basking in pleasant temperatures and abundant sunshine, winter is an excellent time to visit Sarasota. During these months, the city enjoys comfortably mild temperatures ranging from the low 70s to the mid-70s°F (21-24°C) during the day, with cool evenings in the low 50s°F (10-12°C). This season is perfect for enjoying the breathtaking beaches, exploring the cultural scene, and engaging in various outdoor activities. Winter is also a prime time for witnessing the annual Sarasota Winter Fine Art Festival and attending performances at the Sarasota Opera House.

Spring (March to May)

As nature awakens and vibrant flowers bloom, spring casts its enchantment upon Sarasota. With daytime temperatures ranging from the high 70s to low 80s°F (25-28°C) and pleasantly cool evenings in the mid-60s°F (18-20°C), this season is ideal for immersing yourself in the city's natural beauty and attending outdoor festivals and events. Spring offers a wonderful opportunity to explore Sarasota's parks and gardens, partake in water activities, and embrace the city's lively arts and culture scene. The Sarasota Film Festival and the Ringling International Arts Festival are just a couple of the highlights you can look forward to during this time.

Summer (June to August)

If you're seeking sun-soaked adventures and the delights of beachside relaxation, summer is a splendid time to visit Sarasota. The days are warm, with temperatures ranging from the high 80s to low 90s°F (31-33°C), while evenings offer a welcome respite with temperatures in the mid-70s°F (24-26°C). Summer brings a burst of vibrant energy to the city, with an array of water sports, outdoor concerts, and lively events, such as the Sarasota Music Festival and the Siesta Key Crystal Classic Sand Sculpting Competition. While occasional afternoon thunderstorms can occur, they pass quickly, leaving the air refreshed and ready for further exploration.

Fall (September to November)

As summer gradually fades away, fall ushers in a sense of tranquility in Sarasota. Daytime temperatures range from the high 70s to low 80s°F (25-28°C), while evenings cool down to the mid-60s°F (18-20°C). This season offers a delightful combination of pleasant weather, fewer crowds, and the opportunity to witness nature's autumnal transformation. Fall is the perfect time to discover Sarasota's parks and nature preserves, enjoy al fresco dining, and delve into the city's rich cultural heritage. The Sarasota Chalk Festival and the Ringling International Arts Festival are just a few of the events that showcase the city's creative spirit during this time.

As you plan your visit to Sarasota, consider the experiences you seek and the climate that best aligns with your preferences. Each season has its allure, from the delightful mildness of winter to the sun-soaked adventures of summer. Take into account the various festivals and events that occur throughout the year, as they add an extra layer of excitement to your exploration of Sarasota.

Visa and Travel Requirements

It is essential to familiarize yourself with the visa and travel requirements to ensure a smooth and hassle-free experience when traveling to Sarasota Florida. I have gathered key information to guide you through this process and provide you with the necessary information to plan your visit.

Visa Requirements

If you are a citizen of one of the 39 visa waiver countries participating in the Visa Waiver Program (VWP), you may be eligible to travel to Sarasota, Florida without obtaining a visa before arrival. Citizens from countries such as the United Kingdom, Germany, Japan, and Australia, among others, can enter the United States for tourism or business purposes for up to 90 days without a visa.

For travelers from countries not included in the Visa Waiver Program, a valid visitor visa must be obtained. The B-2 tourist visa is the most common visa category for leisure travel to the United States. It is important to apply for this visa well in advance of your intended travel dates. Contact the nearest U.S. embassy or consulate in your home country to familiarize yourself with the application process, requirements, and any additional documentation needed.

Travel Documents

Regardless of your eligibility for the Visa Waiver Program or the requirement of a visitor visa, certain travel documents are essential to enter the United States. These include:

A valid passport: Ensure that your passport is valid for at least six months beyond your intended departure date from the United States.

Electronic System for Travel Authorization (ESTA): If you are traveling under the Visa Waiver Program, it is mandatory to complete the ESTA application online. The ESTA approval, valid for two years or until your passport expires, authorizes your travel to the United States.

Note: Even if you are eligible for the Visa Waiver Program, it is advisable to confirm your ESTA status before making travel arrangements, as changes in circumstances may affect your eligibility.

Customs and Security

Upon arrival in Sarasota, Florida, you will go through immigration and customs processes. Be prepared to present the necessary travel documents, including your valid passport and, if applicable, your approved ESTA or visitor visa.

Additionally, it is crucial to familiarize yourself with the Transportation Security Administration (TSA) guidelines for air travel. Ensure that you adhere to the rules and regulations regarding carry-on and checked baggage, prohibited items, and any restrictions on liquids, gels, or aerosols.

Travel Insurance

It is highly recommended to obtain travel insurance before embarking on your trip to Sarasota, Florida. Travel insurance can provide coverage for unexpected events such as medical emergencies, trip cancellations, baggage loss, or travel delays. Review different insurance options and choose a policy that suits your specific needs to have peace of mind throughout your journey.

Budgeting and Cost Considerations

Transportation

One of the main expenses to consider is transportation. If you are traveling from a distant location, compare prices for flights to nearby airports to find the most cost-effective option. Additionally, research different airlines, use fare comparison websites, and consider flexible travel dates to secure the best airfare deals.

Upon arrival, you will need to factor in transportation within Sarasota. Public transportation options, such as buses and trolleys, provide affordable means of getting around the city. Alternatively, renting a car may give you more flexibility, but be sure to include the cost of gas and parking fees in your budget.

Accommodation

Sarasota boasts a wide range of accommodation options, ranging from luxurious beachfront resorts to budget-friendly hotels and vacation rentals. To optimize your budget, consider booking accommodation well in advance and explore different options. Websites and apps that compare hotel prices can assist you in finding the most competitive rates. Furthermore, choosing accommodations on the outskirts of the city or during off-peak seasons can often result in significant savings.

Dining and Entertainment

Food and entertainment expenses make up a significant portion of any travel budget. Sarasota offers a diverse culinary scene, with options to suit various tastes and budgets. Consider allocating a per diem for meals and explore a mix of local eateries, seafood shacks, and high-end restaurants to experience the city's gastronomic delights.

When it comes to entertainment, Sarasota provides a wealth of cultural attractions and outdoor activities. Research the cost of admission to museums, art galleries, and performances, and plan your itinerary accordingly. Additionally, take advantage of the city's beautiful parks, public beaches, and natural attractions, which often come with minimal or no admission fees.

Excursions and Tours

Sarasota and its surrounding areas offer numerous excursions and tours, allowing you to immerse yourself in the region's natural beauty and unique experiences. Whether it's a boat ride to spot dolphins, kayaking through mangroves, or visiting the famous Ringling Museum, be sure to account for these potential expenses when crafting your budget. Research different tour operators and compare prices to find the best deal without compromising the quality of your experience.

Miscellaneous Expenses

Remember to be prepared for unforeseen expenses that might crop up during your journey. Set aside a small buffer in your budget to account for unforeseen costs, emergencies, or those spontaneous moments when an opportunity presents itself that you simply cannot resist.

By carefully considering transportation, accommodation, dining, entertainment, excursions, and miscellaneous expenses, you can formulate a realistic budget for your trip to Sarasota. Remember to track your expenditures during your stay to ensure you adhere to your budget and make the most of your time in this captivating coastal city.

Travel Essentials

Travel Documents

Ensure you have all the required travel documents neatly organized and easily accessible throughout your journey. These documents may include:

- Valid passport: Check that your passport is not expired, and it has a validity of at least six months beyond your intended departure date from the United States.
- Visa or ESTA Approval: If applicable, carry your visitor visa or ESTA approval documents as required.
- Airline tickets: Print out or have digital copies of your flight itineraries for ease of reference.
- Travel insurance documents: Keep a copy of your travel insurance policy and any relevant contact information readily available.
- Identification cards: Carry a government-issued identification card to use for any required identification purposes during your trip.

Money and Payment Methods

It is essential to have a secure and convenient way to carry and access money during your travels. Consider the following:

- Local currency: Carry a reasonable amount of local currency or plan to exchange currency upon arrival in Sarasota. It is advisable to have some smaller bills for convenience.
- Credit/debit cards: Carry at least one credit or debit card for use at hotels, restaurants, and shops. Make sure that your card is internationally accepted and notify your bank about your travel arrangements to prevent any possible complications.
- Emergency cash: Keep a small emergency cash reserve separate from your primary funds, stored in a safe and discreet location.

Clothing and Accessories

Pack appropriate clothing and accessories based on the time of year and activities you plan to engage in during your visit to Sarasota. Consider the following:

- Lightweight and breathable clothing: Sarasota's subtropical climate calls for comfortable attire suitable for warm weather. Pack lightweight tops, shorts, lightweight pants, dresses, and swimsuits.
- Layers and cover-ups: Despite the warm temperatures, it is advisable to bring along light layers, such as a cardigan or a light jacket, as indoor establishments might have air conditioning.
- Comfortable footwear: Be prepared with comfortable walking shoes for exploring the city, as well as sandals or flip-flops for excursions to the beach.
- Sun protection: Sarasota's sunny climate demands adequate sun protection. Pack sunscreen with a high SPF, a wide-brimmed hat, sunglasses, and a lightweight scarf or cover-up for added sun protection.
- Rain gear: Depending on the time of year, an umbrella or a lightweight rain poncho may come in handy during sudden rain showers.

Electronics and Other Essentials

Consider these additional essentials to make your trip more convenient and enjoyable:

- Mobile phone and charger: Ensure your mobile phone is fully charged and bring along a charger and a plug adaptor suitable for use in the United States.
- Travel adapter: If you are bringing electronic devices with different plug types, a universal travel adapter will ensure you can charge and use your electronics without any issues.
- Portable power bank: Keep a portable power bank handy to recharge your mobile devices while on the go.
- Medications: If you are taking any prescription medications, be sure to bring an ample supply for the duration of your trip. It is also advisable to carry a copy of your prescription in case any issues arise.
- Toiletries: Pack travel-sized toiletries, including shampoo, conditioner, toothpaste, toothbrush, and any specific personal hygiene items you require.

- Travel guidebook or electronic app: Consider bringing a travel guidebook or downloading a travel app specific to Sarasota to enhance your exploration of the city.

By ensuring you have all the necessary travel essentials, you can enjoy a more comfortable and stress-free visit to Sarasota. Remember to pack efficiently, and leave room for any souvenirs.

Chapter 2: Getting There

Transportation Options

There are various transportation options available to help you reach the captivating city of Sarasota. Whether you are arriving from a nearby location or from across the globe, understanding these different ways to travel will ensure a smooth and convenient journey. Let's delve into the transportation options that await you:

Air Travel

If you're traveling from distant locations, air travel is often the most efficient and time-saving option. Sarasota-Bradenton International Airport (SRQ) serves as the main gateway to the region, offering domestic and international flights. Several major airlines operate regular flights to SRQ, providing you with a multitude of options to choose from. Upon landing at SRQ, you will find convenient ground transportation options, including taxis, ride-sharing services, and car rental agencies, allowing you to easily reach your destination in Sarasota.

Driving

If you prefer the freedom and flexibility of driving, Sarasota can be easily accessed via well-maintained roadways. Interstate 75 (I-75) is the main highway connecting Sarasota to various cities and states in the region. If you are arriving from the north, I-75 provides a direct route from places such as Tampa, Orlando, and even as far as Atlanta. Alternatively, consider scenic drives along the Gulf Coast, which offer breathtaking views and charming towns along the way. If you choose to drive to Sarasota, be sure to be familiar with any toll roads and plan accordingly for fuel stops and rest breaks. Keep in mind that parking may be limited in certain areas, so choose, in advance, an accommodation option that offers free parking space.

Train and Bus Travel

While train travel may not be as popular in the United States as it is in some other countries, it is still a viable option to reach Sarasota. Amtrak operates several routes that pass through Florida, including stops in nearby cities such as Tampa and Orlando. From these cities, you can easily connect to Sarasota via other transportation options. Additionally, Greyhound and other bus companies offer intercity bus services, providing an affordable alternative if you prefer not to drive or fly. The bus stations in Tampa and Orlando are the main hubs for travel to Sarasota, with frequent routes available.

Cruise Ships

If you're looking for a unique and enjoyable way to arrive in Sarasota, cruise ships present an enticing option. Port Tampa Bay, located approximately an hour's drive from Sarasota, serves as a departure point for various cruise lines. Embarking on a cruise not only allows you to enjoy luxurious accommodations and exciting onboard activities but also provides the opportunity to explore multiple destinations before reaching Sarasota. Once in Sarasota, various transportation options, including shuttles and taxis, can take you to your final destination, allowing you to enjoy all the wonders this charming coastal city has to offer.

Public Transportation

Once you arrive in Sarasota, the city provides public transportation options to explore its many attractions. Sarasota offers a network of buses and trolleys that can take you to popular destinations within the city and its surroundings. Public transportation is a convenient and cost-effective way to get around if you prefer not to drive or rent a car. Additionally, rideshare services such as Uber and Lyft operate in Sarasota, providing you with another option for getting around the city.

Consider factors such as travel time, convenience, budget, and personal preferences when selecting your mode of transportation to Sarasota. Each option has its unique advantages, so choose the one that best aligns with your needs.

Airports and Arrival Information

Sarasota-Bradenton International Airport (SRQ)

Sarasota-Bradenton International Airport serves as the primary gateway for travelers visiting the city of Sarasota, offering both domestic and international flights. Located just a short distance from downtown Sarasota, SRQ provides convenient access to the region. The airport features a modern terminal and offers a range of amenities and services to make your journey comfortable. Multiple major airlines, including American Airlines, Delta Air Lines, and United Airlines, operate regular flights to and from SRQ, ensuring a wide range of options. Ground transportation options, such as taxis, ride-sharing services, and car rental agencies, are readily available upon arrival at SRQ, allowing you to reach your desired destination with ease.

Tampa International Airport (TPA)

If you are unable to find a direct flight to Sarasota, or if you prefer more options, Tampa International Airport in nearby Tampa is a convenient alternative. Tampa International Airport is a major hub for domestic and international flights, offering a wide range of airlines and destinations. From Tampa International Airport, you can easily reach Sarasota by renting a car, taking a shuttle service, or utilizing various ground transportation options. The airport also provides excellent facilities, including dining options, shops, and services to ensure a pleasant travel experience.

Southwest Florida International Airport (RSW)

Located in Fort Myers, Southwest Florida International Airport serves as another popular arrival point for travelers coming to the Sarasota area. RSW offers a variety of domestic and international flights, providing additional options for you. From Fort Myers, you can reach Sarasota by car, rental car, or other ground transportation services available at the airport. Similar to the other airports mentioned, RSW provides a range of facilities to make your journey comfortable and enjoyable.

Orlando International Airport (MCO)

If you're planning to explore Orlando and its famed attractions before heading to Sarasota, Orlando International Airport is an ideal choice. As one of the busiest airports in Florida, MCO offers an extensive selection of airlines and destinations. After arriving in Orlando, you can choose from various transportation options to continue your journey to Sarasota, such as rental cars, shuttles, or even domestic flights to SRQ.

It is recommended to book your air travel well in advance to secure the most convenient flight and best fares. Compare prices and find the most suitable options for your trip. Consider factors such as flight times, layovers, and airline reputations to facilitate a seamless and enjoyable travel experience.

Local Transportation in Sarasota

Sarasota County Area Transit (SCAT) Bus Service

The Sarasota County Area Transit (SCAT) offers a comprehensive bus service that serves the city of Sarasota and its surrounding areas. SCAT provides an extensive network of routes, covering key locations and popular destinations. The buses are equipped with modern amenities and are operated by friendly and knowledgeable staff. Using the SCAT bus service is an affordable and environmentally friendly way to explore the city. Fare rates are reasonable, and various pass options are available for frequent travelers. The routes and schedules can be accessed through the SCAT website or mobile app, making it easy to plan your journey.

The Breeze Trolley

For a fun and nostalgic way to get around Sarasota, consider hopping on The Breeze Trolley. The trolley service operates along the popular Sarasota County coastline, connecting various beaches, parks, and attractions. The open-air trolleys provide a charming and scenic ride, allowing you to enjoy the beautiful surroundings. The Breeze Trolley operates on a regular schedule and offers affordable fares, making it an excellent option for beachgoers and sightseers.

Ride-Sharing Services

Popular ride-sharing services such as Uber and Lyft operate within Sarasota, providing an efficient and convenient way to get around the city. With just a few taps on your smartphone, you can easily request a ride and be on your way to your desired destination. Ride-sharing services offer flexible pick-up and drop-off locations, allowing you to explore Sarasota at your own pace. These services are available 24/7, ensuring that you have reliable transportation options regardless of the time of day.

Bicycle Rentals

Sarasota is a bike-friendly city with plenty of dedicated bike lanes and paths, making cycling a popular mode of transportation for both locals and visitors. Numerous bike rental shops are located throughout the city, offering a range of bicycles for all ages and skill levels. Renting a bike allows you to explore Sarasota at a leisurely pace while enjoying the scenic views and warm weather. It's a great way to access the stunning beaches, parks, and neighborhoods that make Sarasota unique.

Car Rental

If you prefer the convenience and flexibility of having your vehicle, car rentals are available in Sarasota. Multiple rental agencies operate within the city, offering a wide selection of vehicles to suit your preferences. Renting a car provides you with the freedom to explore Sarasota and its surrounding areas at your own pace. Keep in mind that parking may be limited in certain areas, so it's advisable to check for parking options near your accommodations or attractions of interest.

These local transportation options in Sarasota ensure that you can navigate the city efficiently and comfortably. With this comprehensive information about the transportation options in and around Sarasota, you are now well-equipped to plan your journey and arrive smoothly at your destination.

Chapter 3: Top Attractions in Sarasota

Cultural and Historical Attractions

The Ringling Museum of Art

As you approach the majestic grounds of The Ringling Museum of Art, located at 5401 Bay Shore Road, Sarasota, you are stepping into a realm where art and history converge spectacularly. Founded by John Ringling, one of the famed Ringling Brothers of circus renown, this museum is not only a tribute to his love for art but also a cornerstone of cultural enrichment in Sarasota.

Location and Address

Nestled on the picturesque Sarasota Bay, The Ringling Museum of Art boasts a sprawling estate that is a feast for the eyes even before you enter its galleries. The official address is 5401 Bay Shore Road, Sarasota, Florida. The museum is part of the larger Ringling estate, which includes the Ca' d'Zan Mansion, the Circus Museum, and the Historic Asolo Theater, all spread out over 66 acres of lush gardens and waterfront views.

How to Get There

Getting to The Ringling Museum of Art is straightforward, whether you're driving or using public transport. If you're coming from downtown Sarasota, you can take U.S. Route 41 north until you reach University Parkway, then head west towards the bay. The museum is just a short drive from there. Alternatively, several bus routes service the area, with stops conveniently located near the entrance of the museum, ensuring that it is accessible to everyone.

Exploring the Diverse Collections

Upon entering the museum, you find yourself immersed in an extensive collection that spans continents and centuries. The museum's European paintings, including masterpieces by Velázquez, Poussin, and Veronese, are some of the most admired in the United States. You'll wander through galleries filled with significant works of art that transport you from the Renaissance to the Baroque period, and into the modern era.

The Asian art collection showcases the depth and breadth of artistic achievements from cultures across Asia, with artifacts that include delicate porcelain, intricate sculptures, and bold paintings. These pieces not only highlight individual craftsmanship but also tell the broader story of Asia's rich cultural heritage.

Experiencing the Exhibitions

The Ringling Museum of Art is dynamic, with temporary exhibitions that are as compelling as its permanent collection. These exhibitions are carefully curated to both complement and challenge the mainstays of the museum's collection, offering fresh perspectives and new contexts. From cutting-edge contemporary art to historical retrospectives, each exhibit is designed to provoke thought and inspire awe.

One such example is the modern circus posters exhibit, which connects directly to John Ringling's legacy in the circus industry. This exhibit not only displays vibrant and colorful posters but also explores the circus's impact on popular culture and the arts.

Impact on the Local Art Scene

The Ringling Museum of Art serves as a hub for the artistic community in Sarasota. It plays a pivotal role in the local culture by offering educational programs, artist talks, and special events that engage the community and foster a deeper appreciation for the arts. The museum's commitment to accessibility and education is evident in its outreach programs, which extend well beyond its walls to schools and community centers across the region.

Preserving John Ringling's Legacy

More than just a museum, this institution stands as a lasting testament to John Ringling's vision and his extraordinary commitment to both the arts and the community of Sarasota. His legacy is preserved not only through the art collected during his lifetime but also through the museum's ongoing efforts to enhance and expand its collections.

John Ringling's influence is perhaps most palpable in the Ca' d'Zan Mansion, a part of the estate that reflects his style and passion for

Venetian Gothic architecture. The mansion, meticulously restored, offers a glimpse into the life of the Ringlings, adorned with original furnishings and art from their extensive travels.

Historic Spanish Point

Nestled in the lush landscape of Osprey, Florida, Historic Spanish Point offers a unique glimpse into 5,000 years of Florida history. This 30-acre museum and environmental complex provides an unparalleled opportunity to explore prehistoric shell mounds, pioneer-era buildings, and beautifully preserved gardens, making it a must-visit for history enthusiasts and nature lovers alike.

Location and Address

Historic Spanish Point is located at 337 North Tamiami Trail, Osprey, Florida. This historic site sits along the shores of Little Sarasota Bay, offering scenic views and a serene atmosphere that enhances its historical explorations.

How to Get There

Reaching Historic Spanish Point is an easy drive from downtown Sarasota, approximately 10 miles south along the Tamiami Trail (US-41). If you're relying on public transportation, Sarasota County Area Transit (SCAT) provides bus services that stop near the entrance of the museum. Coming from further afield, the proximity of this attraction to major highways makes it accessible from other parts of Florida.

Exploring the Archaeological Features

One of the highlights of Historic Spanish Point is its extensive archaeological record that delves deep into the region's history. The site is home to one of the largest preserved and accessible shell mounds on the Gulf Coast, known as middens, created by the Native American inhabitants of the region thousands of years ago. These mounds are not only impressive in their size and preservation but also offer insights into the daily lives, diets, and environments of the early peoples who built them.

You can walk through the Prehistoric Mound Exhibit, an innovative display that cuts through a shell midden to reveal layers of history built up over centuries. This exhibit provides a tangible connection to the past, showcasing tools, pottery, and remnants of the region's first inhabitants.

Pioneer-Era Buildings and Their Stories

Historic Spanish Point also chronicles a more recent history with its pioneer-era buildings. The Webb/Burns Point Homestead area includes the 1901 Guptill House, which shows how early 20th-century settlers adapted to and thrived in the Florida landscape. The Mary's Chapel and Pioneer Cemetery add depth to the story, offering a poignant look at the spiritual and communal life of the area's settlers.

The highlight is the White Cottage, built in 1893 as part of the original Webb homestead. Here, you can immerse yourself in the Webb family's history, understanding their significant role in developing the area during the homesteading era. Each building is carefully preserved, allowing you to step back in time and experience the rustic charm and resilience of pioneer life.

Gardens and Grounds

Beyond its historical and archaeological significance, Historic Spanish Point is renowned for its stunning gardens, which were designed in the early 20th century by Mrs. Potter Palmer, a prominent Chicago socialite and the widow of Bertha Honoré Palmer, a significant figure in Sarasota's development. The Sunken Garden, Duchene Lawn, and Jungle Walk each offer unique botanical experiences that blend the natural beauty of Florida with careful landscaping inspired by the aesthetics of the time.

The Impact on Local History

Historic Spanish Point not only preserves these artifacts and buildings but also actively interprets them, offering educational programs that discuss the environmental and cultural history of the region. It serves as a crucial educational resource, illuminating Sarasota's history from its earliest days through to its development into the vibrant community it is today.

Ca d'Zan Mansion

A testament to the grandeur and spirit of the American Gilded Age, the Ca d'Zan Mansion stands as a pivotal piece of Sarasota's architectural and cultural heritage. This palatial residence was once the winter home of John and Mable Ringling, of the famed Ringling Bros. Circus. Today, it serves not only as a window into the opulent lifestyle of one of America's most influential couples but also as a key player in the cultural development of Sarasota.

Location and Address

The Ca d'Zan Mansion is located on the grounds of The Ringling estate at 5401 Bay Shore Road, Sarasota, FL 34243. Situated along the picturesque Sarasota Bay, the mansion is part of the larger Ringling Museum complex, which includes the Art Museum, Circus Museum, and the Historic Asolo Theater.

How to Get There

Accessing Ca d'Zan is straightforward. From downtown Sarasota, take US-41 North towards the Sarasota-Bradenton International Airport. Turn right onto University Parkway and then left onto Bay Shore Road. Signage for The Ringling and Ca d'Zan will guide you to the visitor parking areas. Public transportation options are available, with bus routes stopping near the entrance of The Ringling, making it accessible if you prefer not to drive.

Architectural Marvel

Designed by New York architect Dwight James Baum in the Venetian Gothic style, Ca d'Zan, which means "House of John" in Venetian dialect, is an emblem of luxury and creativity. Its façade is adorned with terra cotta tiles and intricate stonework, echoing the grand palazzos of Venice, Italy. The mansion spans an impressive 36,000 square feet, with each room bearing unique artistic details that reflect the Ringlings' travels and tastes.

The opulence is most vivid in the grand court, with its high ceilings, stained glass windows, and detailed marble flooring. This space was designed both to awe and to serve as a fitting backdrop for the lavish entertainment style of its owners. The residence's exterior is equally striking, featuring a waterfront terrace that offers stunning views of Sarasota Bay, framed by classical balustrades and decorative sculptures.

Historical Context

Built between 1924 and 1926, during the height of the Florida land boom, Ca d'Zan reflects the prosperity and the ambitious spirit of the era. It was here that John Ringling, realizing the potential of Sarasota as a luxury tourist destination, decided to invest heavily. His influence was instrumental in transforming Sarasota from a quiet fishing town into a cultural and social hotspot.

The mansion also served as a venue for many of the Ringlings' social gatherings, attracting celebrities, artists, and business tycoons from around the country. These events were more than mere social occasions; they helped forge Sarasota's identity as a cultural nucleus, attracting other investors and cultural figures to the region.

Influence on Sarasota's Development

John Ringling's decision to make Sarasota the winter quarters for the Ringling Bros. and Barnum & Bailey Circus brought an economic and cultural boost to the area. Ca d'Zan became a symbol of this new era of prosperity and was pivotal in elevating Sarasota's status on the national stage. The legacy of the Ringlings encapsulated within the walls of Ca d'Zan, continued to shape the cultural landscape of Sarasota long after their deaths.

The mansion not only attracted tourism but also inspired a wave of architectural and artistic endeavors in the area, contributing to Sarasota's reputation as a center for the arts and culture. This influence is still evident today, as the city continues to thrive as a vibrant arts community.

Sarasota Opera House

Stepping into the Sarasota Opera House is like entering a realm where history, culture, and artistic excellence converge. Known for its intimate ambiance and exceptional acoustics, the Opera House has been a cornerstone of Sarasota's cultural landscape since its inception. As one of the city's most cherished historical landmarks, it offers a glimpse into the rich artistic heritage and vibrant community spirit that characterize Sarasota.

Location and Address

Located in the heart of downtown Sarasota at 61 North Pineapple Avenue, Sarasota, FL 34236, the Sarasota Opera House is nestled among art galleries, restaurants, and boutiques, making it a central figure in the city's bustling cultural scene.

How to Get There

Getting to the Sarasota Opera House is straightforward, given its prominent location in downtown Sarasota. If driving, you can access the area via Main Street or Fruitville Road, with several parking options available nearby, including street parking and public lots. If you prefer public transit, multiple bus lines run through downtown Sarasota, with stops conveniently close to the Opera House. The central location also makes it accessible by foot or bike if you're staying in downtown Sarasota.

Architectural Beauty

Originally built in 1926 as the Edwards Theatre, the building was crafted in the Mediterranean Revival style that was popular in Florida during the early 20th century. The facade is adorned with classical columns, ornate detailing, and a charming marquee. The interior of the Opera House is equally impressive, featuring opulent decorations, such as chandeliers, a grand staircase, and a beautifully adorned auditorium with seating that allows every guest a perfect view of the stage.

The Opera House underwent significant renovations in 2008, which preserved its historical integrity while updating its facilities to modern standards. These renovations included enhancing the stage's functionality and the auditorium's comfort, ensuring that the Opera House remains a state-of-the-art venue.

Historical Performances and Legacy

Since its transformation into an opera house in 1979, the venue has hosted an array of performances, becoming the official home of the Sarasota Opera in 1984. The Opera House is renowned for its Verdi Cycle, a unique project completed in 2016, which aimed to perform every piece of music Giuseppe Verdi ever composed. This ambitious endeavor not only garnered international acclaim but also solidified the Opera House's reputation as a leading institution in the operatic world.

Throughout its history, the Sarasota Opera House has seen performances from some of the most notable names in opera and has been a launchpad for rising stars. Its dedication to high-quality productions and community engagement has made it a beloved institution among locals and a must-visit destination for tourists.

Contribution to the Arts Community

The impact of the Sarasota Opera House on the local arts community cannot be overstated. It is a hub for cultural activity in Sarasota, offering a year-round program that includes opera, concerts, ballets, film festivals, and more. Beyond its role as a performance venue, the Opera House is committed to arts education and community outreach. It hosts numerous educational programs, workshops, and lectures that aim to foster an appreciation for opera and the performing arts within the community.

Each season, the Opera House draws tens of thousands of patrons, not only enriching Sarasota's cultural life but also contributing significantly to its economy. The presence of this institution enhances the city's allure as a cultural destination, attracting visitors from around the globe who come to experience world-class performances in a historic setting.

Sarasota Classic Car Museum

For car enthusiasts and history buffs alike, the Sarasota Classic Car Museum stands as a beacon of automotive heritage, offering a nostalgic journey through the evolution of automobiles. As the second oldest continuously operating antique car museum in the nation, this venue captures the essence of innovation and design that has propelled the automotive industry forward.

Location and Address

The Sarasota Classic Car Museum is conveniently situated at 5500 N Tamiami Trail, Sarasota, Florida. Located near the Sarasota-Bradenton International Airport and just north of downtown Sarasota, it's an easily accessible destination.

How to Get There

Driving to the museum is straightforward, with it being directly off the Tamiami Trail (US-41), making it visible and accessible from one of

Sarasota's main thoroughfares. If you're utilizing public transportation, several bus routes stop near the museum, ensuring that even those without private vehicles can enjoy the collections. Ample parking is available on-site including designated spots for larger vehicles or buses.

The Collection and Unique Exhibits

Upon entering the Sarasota Classic Car Museum, you will be greeted by an impressive array of over 75 automobiles that showcase more than a century of automotive history. The collection rotates regularly, ensuring that every visit can offer something new, even for repeat visitors. From vintage classics of the early 1900s to more modern exotic vehicles, each car is meticulously maintained, preserving its beauty and operational integrity.

The museum is home to an eclectic mix of vehicles, including European classics from the likes of Rolls-Royce and Mercedes-Benz, American muscle cars that epitomize the rugged spirit of the 60s and 70s, and even whimsical custom cars that appear to have leaped straight out of comic books and movies. Notably, the museum features a John Lennon Rolls-Royce, an iconic vehicle associated with one of the most influential musicians of the 20th century.

Highlight Exhibits

One of the standout exhibits is the "Paul McCartney Story," which features a car that was once owned by the Beatles star, accompanied by personal artifacts and stories of the car's history. This exhibit not only appeals to car enthusiasts but also music fans, illustrating the interconnectedness of pop culture and automotive history.

The museum also dedicates a significant portion of its space to Sarasota's automotive history, showcasing how the region contributed to and was influenced by automotive advancements. This includes displays on the early carriages and motor vehicles that facilitated Sarasota's development as a tourist and cultural destination.

Interactive and Educational Experiences

The Sarasota Classic Car Museum is not just about observing; it's about engaging and learning. Interactive displays, including simulators and touch screens, provide you with insights into the engineering marvels behind these classic cars. Educational tours, led by knowledgeable guides, delve deeper into the stories of the cars and their impacts on society and culture throughout the decades.

Events and Community Engagement

Beyond its role as a museum, the venue serves as a community hub, hosting various events throughout the year. From classic car shows where collectors and enthusiasts can display their prized vehicles, to themed nights and private events, the museum fosters a sense of community among those who share a passion for automotive history.

Historical Significance

The Sarasota Classic Car Museum does more than display old cars; it preserves a slice of automotive history that is vital for future generations. Each vehicle in the museum tells a story of technological innovation, cultural shifts, and artistic design. By maintaining these machines, the museum plays a crucial role in educating the public about the significant developments that cars have brought to societal mobility and freedom.

Bishop Museum of Science and Nature

Situated in the heart of Bradenton, just a short drive from Sarasota, the Bishop Museum of Science and Nature stands as the largest natural and cultural history museum on Florida's Gulf Coast. It plays a pivotal role in educating the public about the region's rich biodiversity, its paleontological past, and the conservation efforts crucial for future sustainability.

Location and Address

The Bishop Museum of Science and Nature is located at 201 10th Street West, Bradenton, FL 34205. Nestled in downtown Bradenton, the museum is part of the vibrant cultural landscape of the Sarasota Bay area.

How to Get There

Reaching the Bishop Museum is convenient whether you are coming from Sarasota or farther afield. If driving from Sarasota, take US-41 north to Bradenton, and then follow signs to downtown Bradenton – the museum is just minutes from the Bradenton Riverwalk. Public transportation options are also available, with Manatee County Area

Transit (MCAT) buses servicing the area, ensuring easy access for all visitors.

Exploring Key Exhibits

As you enter the Bishop Museum of Science and Nature, you are greeted by an array of exhibits that promise to educate and fascinate. The museum's hallmark is its Parker Manatee Aquarium, which serves as a rehabilitation center for injured manatees and an educational platform about this gentle giant's habitat and conservation needs. Watching these serene creatures from the underwater viewing area is not just an enchanting experience but also an educational one, emphasizing the fragile ecosystem they inhabit.

Another standout exhibit is the Planetarium, where you can embark on a cosmic journey through the universe. The state-of-the-art system brings the stars and planets to life, offering daily shows that explore various astronomical phenomena. This immersive experience is designed to spark curiosity and wonder about the vastness of space and our place within it.

The museum also takes pride in its extensive fossil collection, which includes the Montague Tallant collection of prehistoric Florida fossils. This exhibit takes you back in time to when giant sharks and saber-toothed cats roamed the region. It not only highlights the area's geological history but also underscores the changes that have occurred over millions of years, shaping the natural world as we know it today.

Educational Programs and Community Engagement

Education is at the core of the Bishop Museum's mission. The institution offers a wide range of programs aimed at different age groups, from young children to adults. These programs include hands-on workshops, summer camps, and field trips that align with STEM (Science, Technology, Engineering, and Math) learning objectives. Each program is designed to foster a deeper understanding of science and nature, encouraging students to think critically about environmental issues and conservation.

Furthermore, the museum hosts special events throughout the year, such as guest lectures, temporary exhibits, and community outreach activities that engage the wider public in science and natural history. These events not only enhance the visitor experience but also strengthen community ties by making science accessible and enjoyable for everyone.

Conservation Efforts

The Bishop Museum of Science and Nature is deeply committed to conservation and research. Through its various initiatives, the museum works closely with local and national organizations to promote wildlife conservation and environmental education. The manatee rehabilitation facility, for example, not only helps injured manatees recover but also serves as a research center for studying their behavior and health, contributing valuable data to conservation efforts.

Beaches and Natural Attractions

Siesta Key Beach

Siesta Key Beach, renowned for its stunning natural beauty and exceptional qualities, stands out as a prime attraction in Sarasota, Florida. Often ranked among the best beaches in the United States, Siesta Key Beach offers a unique blend of geological features and recreational activities that draw visitors from all over the world.

Location and Address

Siesta Key Beach is located on Siesta Key, a barrier island off the coast of Sarasota, Florida. The physical address is 948 Beach Rd, Siesta Key, Florida

Getting There

Reaching Siesta Key Beach is straightforward. If you're traveling from Sarasota, you can take Route 41 to Stickney Point Road, which leads directly to the beach. Public transportation options include Sarasota County Area Transit (SCAT) buses that provide routes to Siesta Key. If you're flying in, the nearest airport is Sarasota-Bradenton International Airport, from which you can rent a car or take a taxi for the short drive to the beach.

Unique Geological Features

What sets Siesta Key Beach apart are its remarkable sand qualities. Unlike most beaches that are composed of crushed coral, the sand at Siesta Key Beach is 99% quartz. This fine quartz sand originated from the Appalachian Mountains, carried down to the Gulf by rivers over millennia. Its pure quartz composition gives the sand a fine, powdery texture that is soft to the touch and stays cool underfoot, even under the scorching sun.

This remarkable sand not only contributes to the aesthetic appeal of Siesta Key but also affects the beach's temperature, making it comfortable for visitors to walk barefoot. The reflective nature of the quartz sand also means it's more resistant to heating, ensuring a cooler walking surface compared to the typical darker sands of many other beaches.

Reputation as a Top Beach

The unique qualities of Siesta Key Beach have not gone unnoticed. It has received numerous accolades over the years, including being named the #1 Beach in America by Dr. Beach in 2011, 2015, and 2017. The criteria for these accolades are based on water and sand quality, safety, and environmental management. Siesta Key's clean, clear waters and well-maintained environment make it a safe and appealing destination for families, beach enthusiasts, and nature lovers alike.

In addition to its geological and recreational qualities, Siesta Key Beach is equipped with a range of amenities including lifeguard towers, picnic areas, volleyball courts, and concession stands, enhancing the beach-going experience for all visitors. The beach also hosts various events throughout the year, from sand sculpting competitions to beach runs, adding to its vibrant community atmosphere.

Environmental Considerations and Preservation

The community around Siesta Key Beach is deeply committed to preserving its natural beauty. Efforts include regular beach clean-ups and initiatives to protect local wildlife, particularly sea turtles, which nest on the beach from May through October. These environmental efforts ensure that Siesta Key Beach remains a pristine and inviting destination for future generations.

Siesta Key Beach exemplifies the perfect blend of natural beauty and thoughtful preservation, making it a must-visit destination in Sarasota, Florida. Whether you are a geology enthusiast intrigued by its quartz sands, a family looking for a safe place to play and relax, or a visitor eager to experience one of America's finest beaches, Siesta Key offers an unparalleled beach experience.

Lido Key Beach

Located just west of the vibrant downtown of Sarasota, Lido Key Beach is a haven that combines serene natural beauty with a variety of recreational activities. This beach is a popular destination for both locals and tourists, offering a quieter alternative to the bustling Siesta Key Beach.

Location and How to Get There

Lido Key Beach is situated on Lido Key, a barrier island off the coast of Sarasota. The address for Lido Key Beach is 400 Benjamin Franklin Dr, Sarasota, Florida. You can reach Lido Key by car from downtown Sarasota in about 10 minutes via John Ringling Blvd, which is the main road leading to the Key and continues as Benjamin Franklin Drive at the beach area. Public transportation is also available with Sarasota County Area Transit (SCAT) offering routes that service Lido Key.

Natural Environment

The natural environment of Lido Key Beach is characterized by its gentle, white sand and relatively calm waters, making it an excellent spot for swimming, sunbathing, and shell collecting. The beach is surrounded by Australian pines which provide a natural windbreak and shade, creating a perfect setting for picnics and relaxed afternoons. The presence of these trees also contributes to the beach's unique ecosystem, supporting local wildlife including birds and marine life.

Lido Key's proximity to the Gulf of Mexico influences its marine conditions, which are ideal for various water sports. The beach extends to several miles and includes a designated area at its northern tip known as North Lido Beach, which is more secluded and less developed, offering a more private beach experience and opportunities for bird watching and quiet strolls.

Recreational Activities

Lido Key Beach is renowned for its recreational offerings. You can enjoy kayaking and paddleboarding, available through local rental services that provide all necessary equipment. The calm waters of the Gulf make this location ideal for beginners. Fishing is another popular activity, with several spots along the beach known for being fruitful.

If you prefer land-based activities, the beach features volleyball courts and a playground, making it family-friendly. The nearby Lido Key Nature Park offers walking trails and an opportunity to learn about the local flora and fauna, enhancing ecological appreciation.

Popularity Among Locals and Tourists

The popularity of Lido Key Beach among both locals and tourists can be attributed to its diverse attractions that cater to a variety of interests. Its less commercial and more laid-back atmosphere is particularly appealing to those who seek a quieter beach day. Additionally, its proximity to St. Armands Circle, with its chic boutiques, fine restaurants, and entertainment options, allows you to combine a beach day with shopping and dining, making Lido Key Beach a comprehensive destination.

Cultural and Community Events

Lido Key Beach is not only a natural and recreational haven but also a cultural hotspot. The beach hosts several community events throughout the year, including beach runs, environmental clean-ups, and educational programs about wildlife and marine conservation. These events are often well-attended, strengthening the community spirit and raising awareness about environmental issues.

Myakka River State Park

One of Florida's oldest and largest state parks, Myakka River State Park, offers a spectacular glimpse into a diverse natural environment. This expansive park, which covers 37,000 acres, is famous for its rich wildlife, stunning landscapes, and varied recreational activities, making it a favorite among nature enthusiasts, hikers, bird watchers, and photographers.

Location and How to Get There

Myakka River State Park is located at 13208 State Road 72, Sarasota, Florida. It is approximately 9 miles east of Interstate 75, making it easily accessible by car from Sarasota. If you're arriving by plane, the nearest major airport is Sarasota-Bradenton International Airport, from where you can rent a car and reach the park in about 30 minutes.

Diverse Ecosystems

The park's extensive area encompasses a variety of ecosystems, including wetlands, prairies, hammocks, and pinelands. This diversity contributes to the rich tapestry of plant and animal life within the park. Myakka's river and two lakes provide ample wetlands, attracting numerous species of waterfowl and aquatic wildlife, while the dry prairie areas are known for their seasonal bloom of wildflowers.

Wildlife

Myakka is home to a vast array of wildlife. It is not uncommon to spot American alligators, an iconic symbol of Florida, sunning themselves along the riverbank or silently gliding through the water. The park is also a habitat for many deer, wild turkeys, and feral pigs. Rare sightings include the elusive Florida panther and the bobcat. Birding enthusiasts will delight in the opportunity to observe a spectacular array of birds, including ospreys, eagles, and the colorful roseate spoonbill, among the over 100 species that frequent the park.

Hiking and Trails

With over 39 miles of hiking trails, Myakka River State Park is a hiker's paradise. The trails range from easy walks to strenuous hikes through backcountry areas. One of the most popular trails is the Canopy Walkway, which offers a unique perspective of the park from above the treetops. This suspension bridge and tower provide a panoramic view of the surrounding area, perfect for photography and wildlife observation.

Bird Watching and Photography

For bird watchers, Myakka River State Park is a premier destination. The Birdwalk, a boardwalk stretching out over the Upper Myakka Lake, offers a prime spot for observing water birds in their natural habitat. Photography enthusiasts will find the early morning light particularly magical for capturing the stunning landscape and its inhabitants. The park's diverse scenery and wildlife make it an ideal location for nature photography.

Boating and Fishing

Myakka River and the Upper and Lower Myakka Lakes offer excellent opportunities for boating and fishing. You can rent kayaks and canoes to explore these waterways at a leisurely pace or bring your boats for a more extensive journey down the river. Fishing enthusiasts can try their luck at catching largemouth bass, catfish, and bluegill.

Educational Programs and Tours

The park also offers a variety of educational programs and guided tours, including ranger-led walks and boat tours on the Myakka River, where you can learn about the area's natural history and wildlife. These tours provide valuable insights into the ecosystems of the park and are a great way to enhance your visit.

Marie Selby Botanical Gardens

Marie Selby Botanical Gardens represents a verdant oasis nestled in the urban heart of Sarasota, Florida, known for its impressive living collection of rare and beautiful tropical plants. This institution is not only a place to wander through lush landscapes but also a renowned center for research, conservation, and education related to botanical sciences.

Location and How to Get There

Marie Selby Botanical Gardens is located at 900 S Palm Ave, Sarasota, FL 34236. It is easily accessible via major Sarasota roadways. If you're traveling from downtown Sarasota, you can reach the gardens in just a few minutes by car or bike, heading south on Mound Street (US 41) and turning right onto S Palm Avenue. If you're relying on public transport, several bus routes stop near the gardens, making it a convenient destination for locals and tourists alike.

Botanical Collections

The gardens boast a specialized collection that focuses on epiphytes—plants that grow on other plants non-parasitically, such as orchids, bromeliads, and gesneriads. These plants, often referred to as "*air plants*," are displayed in a way that mimics their natural tropical and subtropical environments. The conservatory houses one of the most diverse collections of bromeliads in the world, while the Tropical Display House delights visitors with its vibrant collection of orchids.

Marie Selby Botanical Gardens is divided into several smaller gardens, each with its own thematic focus. The Bamboo Garden features an extensive variety of bamboo species, the Banyan Grove showcases majestic banyans that provide a dramatic backdrop, and the Children's

Rainforest Garden offers an engaging experience for young ones with its waterfalls, rope bridges, and tree houses.

Conservation Efforts

As a leader in botanical research, Marie Selby Botanical Gardens places a strong emphasis on the conservation of plant biodiversity, particularly the epiphytes that are most vulnerable to habitat destruction and climate change. The Gardens' research programs involve field studies in remote parts of the world and laboratory work in genetics, aiming to discover and document plant species before they are potentially lost. The institution also participates in global conservation efforts, working with international botanical organizations to promote environmental sustainability.

Role in Research and Public Education

Marie Selby Botanical Gardens is dedicated to advancing public understanding of botany with its various educational programs aimed at all ages. The Gardens offer workshops, lectures, and classes that cover a wide range of topics from basic botany to more specialized subjects like plant photography and landscape design. Their commitment to education is perhaps most visible in their interactive exhibits and youth programs, which are designed to inspire a love of nature and an appreciation for the importance of plant conservation.

Educational outreach extends beyond the local community as the Gardens frequently collaborate with academic institutions to provide resources and expertise for botanical research. By hosting scholars and students, Marie Selby Botanical Gardens fosters a learning environment that promotes scientific inquiry and a deeper understanding of the plant kingdom.

Sarasota Jungle Gardens

Sarasota Jungle Gardens stands as one of Sarasota's most unique and interactive attractions, offering you a blend of entertainment, education, and conservation awareness. This family-friendly venue allows guests to experience close encounters with a variety of animals, learn about exotic plants, and enjoy educational shows that emphasize wildlife conservation.

Location and How to Get There

Sarasota Jungle Gardens is located at 3701 Bay Shore Road, Sarasota, Florida. It is easily accessible by car from downtown Sarasota and is only about a 10-minute drive north from the city center. If you're using public transportation, Sarasota County Area Transit (SCAT) provides bus services that stop near the entrance of the gardens, making it convenient if you're without a personal vehicle.

Interactive Experiences

One of the key features of Sarasota Jungle Gardens is its interactive experiences. You have the opportunity to feed flamingos right from their hands, which is one of the only places in the United States where such an interaction is possible. The gardens also offer a petting zoo where children and adults alike can get up close with more domestic animals like goats and sheep.

Another interactive highlight is the famous "Birds of Prey" show which features trained raptors such as eagles, hawks, and owls. These shows not only provide a thrilling experience as birds fly close to the audience but also educate you about the importance of raptors to the ecosystem and the threats they face in the wild.

Educational Value

The educational programs at Sarasota Jungle Gardens are designed to teach you about the behaviors and habitats of the animals within the park. Each show and exhibit explains the conservation status of the species on display and the role that conservation plays in preserving these creatures for future generations. Special educational programs are also available for school groups, which align with Florida's educational standards to help students understand biodiversity and ecological responsibility.

Animal Shows

Sarasota Jungle Gardens is well-known for its entertaining and informative animal shows. The "Reptile Encounter" allows you to learn about various reptiles, both native and exotic. These presentations discuss the ecological roles of reptiles and address common misconceptions about them, often demystifying fears associated with snakes and other less-loved creatures.

Additionally, the "Jungle Trails and Tales" show blends education with entertainment by using humor and audience participation to convey messages about wildlife conservation. The staff at Sarasota Jungle Gardens is adept at engaging audiences of all ages, making learning about conservation both fun and impactful.

Conservation Messages

The overarching theme of Sarasota Jungle Gardens is the importance of preserving natural habitats and the wildlife that inhabits them. The gardens participate in local conservation efforts and educate the public on how they can contribute to environmental stewardship. They highlight the challenges faced by various species due to habitat loss, climate change, and human activity, and they promote ways to mitigate these impacts.

Performing Arts and Entertainment

Sarasota Ballet

The Sarasota Ballet, established in 1987, has grown to become a pivotal part of Sarasota's cultural scene, contributing significantly to the rich tapestry of arts in the region. Under the artistic leadership of Iain Webb, the company has garnered national and international acclaim for its vibrant repertoire and commitment to artistic excellence.

Location and When to Visit

The Sarasota Ballet performs at several venues across Sarasota, including the FSU Center for the Performing Arts, the Sarasota Opera House, and sometimes at the Van Wezel Performing Arts Hall. The ballet season typically runs from October to April, providing a range of performances from classical to contemporary ballet.

Repertoire and Achievements

The repertoire of Sarasota Ballet is diverse, featuring works by major choreographers such as George Balanchine, Frederick Ashton, and Matthew Bourne, alongside new works by contemporary choreographers. This mix offers audiences a rich variety of performances, showcasing the versatility and skill of the company's dancers. One of the standout features of their repertoire is the inclusion of several pieces by Frederick Ashton, which has led Sarasota Ballet to be recognized as a guardian of his works in the U.S.

The company has made significant contributions to the preservation and performance of ballet classics, while also pushing the boundaries of the art form by commissioning new works that explore contemporary themes and narratives. Their performances not only highlight technical excellence but also emphasize expressive, narrative-driven dance, which has been critically acclaimed by audiences and critics alike.

Contribution to the Cultural Landscape

Sarasota Ballet's influence extends beyond just performances. It is deeply integrated into the community through its educational programs and outreach initiatives. The company operates a dance school, the Margaret Barbieri Conservatory, which offers training to young dancers from the local community and from around the world. These programs are crucial for cultivating the next generation of ballet dancers and enthusiasts.

Moreover, the Sarasota Ballet frequently collaborates with local schools, community centers, and other arts organizations to promote the arts and make ballet more accessible to a broader audience. These collaborations often culminate in joint performances, educational workshops, and community events, fostering a strong connection between the arts and the Sarasota community.

International Recognition

Over the years, Sarasota Ballet has achieved a formidable reputation on the international stage. It has been invited to perform at prestigious venues and festivals outside of Florida, including the Kennedy Center in Washington, D.C., and Jacob's Pillow Dance Festival in Massachusetts. These opportunities not only demonstrate the company's high regard in the dance world but also serve to bring Sarasota's vibrant cultural scene to the attention of a global audience.

Van Wezel Performing Arts Hall

In the vibrant cultural scene of Sarasota, the Van Wezel Performing Arts Hall stands out not only as a premier venue for performing arts but also as an architectural landmark. Since its inauguration in 1970, the Hall has played a crucial role in the cultural and social life of Sarasota, attracting world-class performances ranging from music and dance to comedy and Broadway shows.

Architectural Significance

The Van Wezel Performing Arts Hall is renowned for its unique seashell-inspired design, which is both functional and aesthetically pleasing. The distinctive purple exterior and sweeping lines mirror the hall's coastal setting, reflecting the sunsets over Sarasota Bay. This design was the brainchild of the renowned architectural firm Taliesin Associates, founded by Frank Lloyd Wright. The hall's structure is not only designed for visual impact but also acoustical excellence, providing an immersive experience for all attendees.

Location and Access

Located at 777 N Tamiami Trail, Sarasota, Florida, the Van Wezel Performing Arts Hall is situated on the waterfront, making it a picturesque venue for both locals and visitors. It is easily accessible by car and public transportation from major points in downtown Sarasota and surrounding areas.

Diverse Programming

The Van Wezel Performing Arts Hall is known for its diverse programming that caters to a wide array of tastes and preferences. The hall hosts more than 100 events each year, including performances by local arts organizations such as the Sarasota Orchestra, Sarasota Ballet, and the Sarasota Opera. Additionally, it features a broad range of touring attractions, from classical music concerts and operatic performances to popular music shows and stand-up comedy acts.

The programming at Van Wezel is carefully curated to bring the best of the performing arts world to Sarasota. This has included performances by illustrious artists and groups such as Itzhak Perlman, Yo-Yo Ma, the Russian National Ballet, and Broadway touring companies. Each season, the hall strives to offer a balanced mix of performances to ensure something is appealing to everyone in the community.

Role in Attracting World-Class Performances

Van Wezel's reputation as a top-tier performing arts venue is not just due to its striking architecture or prime location, but also its ability to attract high-caliber performances from around the globe. The hall's excellent acoustics, state-of-the-art facilities, and large seating capacity make it an attractive destination for international stars and major touring productions. This has placed Sarasota on the map as a significant cultural hub in Florida, drawing both tourists and art aficionados to the area.

The Van Wezel Performing Arts Hall has significantly contributed to the cultural enrichment of Sarasota. It not only enhances the local arts scene but also catalyzes economic activity, drawing visitors who spend on accommodations, dining, and shopping, thereby benefiting the wider community. The hall's commitment to providing a broad spectrum of entertainment and educational programs makes it a cornerstone of Sarasota's cultural and economic landscape.

Asolo Repertory Theatre

Asolo Repertory Theatre, located in Sarasota, Florida, stands as a cornerstone of the cultural and artistic community. Known for its high-quality theatrical productions and as a major force in American theater, Asolo Rep has a rich history that dates back to its founding in 1959. This venue not only stages a wide variety of plays ranging from bold contemporary works to classical pieces but also serves as a training ground for future theatrical professionals.

Historical Background

The Asolo Repertory Theatre started with the historic Asolo Theater— an 18th-century playhouse originally built in Asolo, Italy. The entire theater was purchased by Ringling Museum's first director, A. Everett "Chick" Austin Jr., and moved piece by piece to Sarasota in the late 1940s. Situated now on the grounds of the Ringling Museum, the Asolo Theater served as the perfect venue to blend European theatrical tradition with American innovation.

Location and Accessibility

The Asolo Repertory Theatre is located at 5555 N Tamiami Trail, Sarasota, Florida, on the campus of the Florida State University Center for the Performing Arts. It is easily accessible by car, with ample parking

44

available for visitors. Public transportation options are also available from different parts of the city.

Seasonal Productions

Each season, Asolo Rep presents a diverse array of productions that include new works, adapted classics, and popular musicals. The theater is well-known for its ambitious programming that often includes Florida premieres and sometimes national premieres, attracting talent from across the nation. Its productions are celebrated for their depth, character study, and ability to engage audiences on multiple levels.

For example, recent seasons have seen a range of productions from classic Shakespeare plays to modern American dramas and transformative musical performances, all of which demonstrate the theater's commitment to artistic excellence and innovation. The winter season typically features a particularly high-profile production, drawing large crowds and garnering substantial local and national attention.

Reputation for Quality

Asolo Repertory Theatre's reputation for quality is reflected in its critical acclaim and the accolades it receives. Known for its masterful production values, the theater employs some of the best in the business—from directors and actors to set designers and costume makers. This dedication to quality ensures that each performance is not only entertaining but also a true work of art.

The theatre also plays a significant role in the community through its educational programs and outreach initiatives. Asolo Rep conducts workshops, hosts school matinees, and engages with various community groups to expand the reach of theatrical arts. These programs emphasize the theatre's commitment to education and accessibility, reinforcing its role as a cultural hub in Sarasota.

Sarasota Orchestra

Founded in 1949, the Sarasota Orchestra has grown to become one of the key drivers of the cultural and artistic landscape in Sarasota, Florida. With its year-round schedule of performances, community engagement initiatives, and educational programs, the orchestra plays a pivotal role in enhancing the cultural life of the community.

Musical Offerings

The Sarasota Orchestra's season includes a diverse range of programming designed to cater to varied musical tastes and preferences. Its offerings include a Masterworks series featuring classic symphonic pieces conducted by distinguished maestros, pop concerts that blend traditional and modern pop music, and Chamber Music concerts that showcase the intimate beauty of ensemble performances.

Special projects and presentations, such as the "Discover Beethoven" series or multimedia performances that integrate video and live narration, also form part of the orchestra's innovative approach. These performances are not only musically enriching but also provide educational value, making classical music accessible and engaging to a broader audience.

Location and Season

The main performances of the Sarasota Orchestra take place at the Van Wezel Performing Arts Hall, located at 777 N Tamiami Trail, Sarasota, Florida. Other venues across the city are also utilized, including the Sarasota Opera House and various community centers, reflecting the orchestra's integration into the fabric of Sarasota.

The season typically runs from September to May, with special summer concerts and community events extending the orchestra's presence throughout the year. This schedule ensures that residents and visitors alike have ample opportunities to experience high-quality live music.

Community Engagement

A core part of the Sarasota Orchestra's mission is its commitment to community engagement and music education. The orchestra runs a comprehensive youth music program, which includes youth orchestras, summer music camps, and school-time concerts designed to inspire the next generation of musicians and music lovers. These programs not only provide high-quality music education but also foster a sense of discipline, creativity, and community among participants.

Outreach initiatives such as free community concerts and performances in non-traditional venues like parks and public spaces are other ways the orchestra connects with the Sarasota community. These events often attract diverse audiences, many of whom might be experiencing orchestral music for the first time.

Impact on Sarasota's Cultural Scene

The presence of the Sarasota Orchestra significantly enriches the cultural fabric of Sarasota. By offering a wide range of musical performances, the orchestra not only entertains but also educates and engages the community, making classical music a vital part of the city's cultural identity. The economic impact is also notable, as concertgoers contribute to the local economy through dining, shopping, and other activities around concert times.

Furthermore, the Sarasota Orchestra's collaborations with other cultural institutions and participation in local festivals and events enhance its role as a cultural ambassador for Sarasota. These collaborations lead to innovative programming and help to build a cohesive cultural community.

Florida Studio Theatre

Located in the heart of downtown Sarasota, Florida Studio Theatre (FST) is renowned for its vibrant contributions to the local cultural scene. Established in 1973, FST has grown from a small touring company to a village of theatres dedicated to developing new plays, presenting contemporary drama, and offering engaging educational programs. This multiplex of performance venues provides a nurturing environment for playwrights and a fascinating cultural destination for visitors and locals alike.

Location and Accessibility

Florida Studio Theatre is conveniently situated at 1241 North Palm Avenue, Sarasota, Florida. The theatre is accessible by public transportation, with nearby stops serviced by Sarasota County Area Transit. If you're driving, there are several parking options available in the vicinity, including street parking and designated lots.

Variety of Plays

FST's commitment to contemporary theatre is evident in its diverse programming, which spans a wide array of genres and styles. The theatre operates on a five-stage complex, where each season includes a mix of plays ranging from cutting-edge new works and musical revues to classic dramas and comedies. This variety ensures that FST has offerings to suit every taste, making it a key player in Sarasota's vibrant arts scene.

The Mainstage Series features larger-scale productions that often include premieres of new plays destined for broader acclaim. Meanwhile, the Cabaret Series is beloved for its innovative musical revues that combine popular music themes with dynamic storytelling. The Stage III Series pushes boundaries even further, often presenting edgier and more experimental works that challenge both the artists and audiences.

Educational Programs

Education is at the core of Florida Studio Theatre's mission. FST's educational initiatives include a wide range of outreach programs, workshops, and classes for all ages. The WRITE A PLAY program is a cornerstone of FST's educational offerings, reaching over 47,000 students annually across numerous states and countries. This program encourages children to write their plays, fostering creativity and writing skills, and culminates in a festival where selected plays written by students are performed.

For adults, the FST School offers classes and workshops in acting, writing, and improvisation taught by professional actors and theatre educators. These programs are designed to cultivate local talent and provide amateurs and aspiring professionals with the skills needed to excel in the performing arts.

Fostering Local Talent

FST plays a crucial role in supporting and nurturing local artistic talent. Through its new play development program, the theatre provides a platform for playwrights to workshop and refine their works, often leading to full productions. Many actors and playwrights have launched or advanced their careers by working with FST, benefiting from its resources, professional exposure, and supportive community.

Community Engagement

Beyond its theatrical productions and educational programs, Florida Studio Theatre is deeply embedded in the Sarasota community. The theatre regularly hosts post-show discussions, panel talks, and community forums that encourage dialogue between artists and audiences. These events serve to deepen the community's engagement with theatre arts and explore the themes and issues presented in FST's productions.

Outdoor and Recreational Activities

Legacy Trail

The Legacy Trail stands as a cornerstone of Sarasota's commitment to outdoor living and recreation. Spanning over 12 miles, this well-maintained trail offers residents and visitors a scenic route that is perfect for biking, walking, jogging, and rollerblading, connecting Sarasota to Venice while traversing diverse natural landscapes.

Location/Address and Accessibility

The Legacy Trail officially starts at Culverhouse Nature Park in Sarasota and extends south to Venice Train Depot in Venice. There are multiple access points along the route, including several parks such as Oscar Scherer State Park and Shamrock Park, which serve as ideal starting points for trail users.

To get there, you can access the northern trailhead at Culverhouse Nature Park, located at 7301 McIntosh Road, Sarasota. Those coming from downtown Sarasota can take US-41 (Tamiami Trail) to Central Sarasota Parkway, then head east to McIntosh Road. Public transportation options are available, with bus routes stopping near several trail access points, making it accessible for everyone without personal vehicles.

Features and Amenities

The Legacy Trail is more than just a path; it is a fully equipped recreational space designed for accessibility and enjoyment. The trail features multiple rest stops, picnic areas, and benches, strategically placed to provide relaxation points for users. Additionally, the trail includes several water stations and restroom facilities, enhancing the convenience for long-distance runners and cyclists.

One of the trail's key features is its wide, paved path that accommodates both casual walkers and competitive cyclists. The smooth pavement is also ideal for wheelchairs and strollers, making it a family-friendly destination for all ages.

Significance to Sarasota's Outdoor Lifestyle

The Legacy Trail is integral to promoting an active and healthy lifestyle in Sarasota. It provides a safe and beautiful environment for outdoor exercise, away from the traffic and noise of the city. On any given day, you can see families on leisurely bike rides, serious cyclists in training, individuals jogging, and nature enthusiasts' bird-watching or enjoying the native flora and fauna.

The trail not only serves as a recreational asset but also as a vital green corridor that supports biodiversity and environmental sustainability. It runs through several habitats, including coastal forests and wetlands, which are crucial for local wildlife. This makes the Legacy Trail a living classroom for environmental education and conservation awareness.

Community and Economic Impact

The Legacy Trail also plays a significant role in enhancing community well-being and economic development. It is a hub for social interactions and community events, such as charity runs, cycling races, and nature walks, which foster community spirit and engagement.

Moreover, the trail boosts local economies by increasing tourism and benefiting businesses near trailheads and access points. Restaurants, bike shops, and other retail establishments near the trail often see increased patronage from trail users looking to refuel or rent equipment.

Nathan Benderson Park

Nathan Benderson Park is a premier multi-use sports venue located in Sarasota, Florida, renowned for its world-class rowing facilities and wide array of community-oriented activities and events. This park has become a hub of recreational and competitive sports, drawing participants and spectators from around the globe.

Location/Address and How to Get There

Nathan Benderson Park is situated at 5851 Nathan Benderson Circle, Sarasota, Florida. The park is easily accessible from Interstate 75, making it straightforward for visitors traveling by car. If you're located in downtown Sarasota, it is approximately a 15-minute drive east. Public transportation options are available, with bus routes servicing the area around the park, ensuring convenient access for everyone.

Facilities and Recreational Uses

The park spans over 600 acres, featuring a 400-acre lake that meets international competition standards, making it one of the few venues in North America capable of hosting world-class rowing events. Beyond rowing, the park offers facilities for a variety of sports, including dragon boat racing, canoe and kayak, triathlons, and more.

For non-competitive recreation, Nathan Benderson Park boasts a playground, picnic pavilions, and a winding trail that encircles the lake, perfect for walking, jogging, and cycling. The park's environment is carefully maintained, featuring pristine landscaping that enhances the natural beauty of the area, making it a popular spot for bird watching and nature photography.

Competitive Uses and Events

Nathan Benderson Park is perhaps best known for its rowing facilities. The park has hosted several prestigious rowing competitions, including the World Rowing Championships, NCAA Rowing Championships, and USRowing Youth National Championships. These events have not only highlighted the park's superb facilities but have also placed Sarasota on the map as an important destination for competitive rowing.

The park's design includes grandstands and other infrastructure to accommodate large numbers of spectators, which is crucial during major events. The availability of such facilities has enabled the park to host other large-scale community events, including concerts, festivals, and sports competitions that go beyond rowing.

Role in Community Engagement

Nathan Benderson Park is deeply integrated into the Sarasota community. The park hosts numerous local events throughout the year, including charity runs, corporate functions, and community gatherings. One of the key aspects of the park is its commitment to accessibility and community involvement. It offers programs that introduce children and adults to rowing, fostering a new generation of enthusiasts and athletes.

The park also serves as a venue for health and wellness programs, providing free or low-cost options for fitness classes and recreational activities. These programs are designed to engage a wide demographic, promoting a healthy lifestyle among the local population.

Economic Impact

Beyond its recreational and sporting functions, Nathan Benderson Park significantly contributes to the local economy. The events hosted at the park draw thousands of visitors who stay in local hotels, dine at local restaurants, and contribute to the economic vitality of Sarasota. The park has been instrumental in boosting tourism, with major sporting events providing national and international exposure.

Big Cat Habitat

Nestled in Sarasota, Florida, the Big Cat Habitat stands as a pivotal institution dedicated to providing a haven for large and exotic animals while promoting wildlife conservation through education and firsthand experiences. This sanctuary is not just a shelter for animals but a center for advocacy and learning, highlighting the critical issues facing these magnificent creatures in the wild and captivity.

Location/Address and Accessibility

Big Cat Habitat is located at 7101 Palmer Blvd, Sarasota, Florida. It is accessible by car via Fruitville Road, one of the main thoroughfares in Sarasota, which connects directly to I-75. This central location makes the sanctuary easily accessible for both locals and visitors. Public transportation options are limited, so driving or taking a taxi is recommended if you're planning a visit.

Mission and Animal Residents

The primary mission of Big Cat Habitat is to rescue and provide a permanent home for exotic and native animals that need refuge. The sanctuary houses a diverse array of species, from big cats like lions, tigers, and leopards to other exotic animals such as bears, primates, and birds. Each animal resident has a unique backstory, often involving rescue from less-than-ideal conditions. By providing these animals with spacious enclosures and enriched environments, the sanctuary ensures their well-being and health.

Educational Programs and Wildlife Conservation Efforts

Education plays a crucial role at Big Cat Habitat. The sanctuary offers a variety of educational programs aimed at all age groups, teaching visitors about the challenges faced by these animals in the wild and the importance of conservation efforts. These programs often include animal demonstrations, keeper talks, and interactive experiences that allow you to learn about animal habits, diets, and conservation status.

The sanctuary's educational outreach extends to local schools and community groups, providing educational presentations and field trip opportunities that foster a deeper understanding and respect for wildlife. These initiatives are designed to inspire a commitment to conservation among the younger generation and the community at large.

Impact on Wildlife Conservation

Big Cat Habitat and Gulf Coast Sanctuary actively participate in broader wildlife conservation efforts, collaborating with international and local organizations to advocate for policies that protect endangered species. Through its rescue efforts, the sanctuary also helps to alleviate the burden on wild populations by providing a refuge for animals that cannot be returned to their natural habitats.

Additionally, the sanctuary's conservation message is amplified through its social media channels and public events, which highlight the plight of exotic animals globally. By educating the public about the illegal wildlife trade and habitat destruction, the sanctuary mobilizes support for conservation initiatives and promotes a more sustainable coexistence with nature.

Celery Fields

Celery Fields stands as a prime example of environmental reclamation and conservation in Sarasota, Florida. Originally utilized for agricultural purposes, this site has been transformed into an important regional stormwater facility and a vibrant sanctuary for wildlife, particularly birds. Its ecological significance and recreational offerings make it a unique and valuable component of Sarasota's outdoor attractions.

Location/Address and How to Get There

Celery Fields is located at 6893 Palmer Blvd, Sarasota, Florida. It is easily accessible from Interstate 75; you can take the Fruitville Road exit and head east until they reach Palmer Blvd, where they turn south. The entrance to Celery Fields is marked and includes ample parking for visitors. This central location, close to major roadways, makes it accessible to both locals and tourists.

Ecological Importance

The primary function of Celery Fields is as a stormwater management facility. It plays a crucial role in mitigating flood risks in the region by collecting and filtering storm runoff, thus protecting the surrounding areas from potential water damage. The design of this facility integrates extensive wetlands, which are crucial for water purification and provide habitat for numerous species.

Beyond its utility for stormwater management, Celery Fields is recognized for its ecological diversity. The site includes a variety of habitats, such as freshwater marshes, ponds, and grasslands. These environments support a rich array of flora and fauna, contributing significantly to local biodiversity.

A Birdwatcher's Paradise

Celery Fields is renowned as one of the best birdwatching spots in southwest Florida. The diverse habitats within the fields attract a wide range of bird species, making it a popular destination for ornithologists and nature enthusiasts. Over 200 species of birds have been documented at Celery Fields, including rare and migratory birds such as the Sandhill Crane, the Bald Eagle, and the Roseate Spoonbill.

The elevated mound in the center of Celery Fields provides panoramic views of the entire area, which is ideal for bird watching and photography. This hill is not only a perfect vantage point but also serves as a peaceful spot for you to enjoy the natural beauty and serenity of the surroundings.

Recreational Activities

Apart from bird watching, Celery Fields offers various recreational activities that promote health and wellness. The extensive network of trails and pathways around the site is perfect for walking, jogging, and cycling. These trails are designed to be accessible for all ages and fitness levels, ensuring that everyone can enjoy the natural beauty of the area.

Additionally, Celery Fields features several boardwalks and observation platforms that allow you to explore the wetlands up close without disturbing the wildlife. These features are especially valuable for educational tours, nature photography, and simply enjoying the tranquil environment.

Community and Educational Impact

Celery Fields also plays a significant role in the community as an educational resource. The site hosts various environmental education programs and workshops that teach participants about wetland ecology, water conservation, and wildlife habitat. These programs are often conducted in collaboration with local schools, universities, and environmental organizations.

Moreover, Celery Fields serves as a model of successful land reclamation and sustainable design. It demonstrates how underutilized or degraded lands can be effectively transformed into valuable ecological assets that serve both environmental and recreational purposes.

The Circus Arts Conservatory

The Circus Arts Conservatory (CAC) in Sarasota, Florida, serves as a vibrant center for circus performance and education, reflecting the city's rich circus heritage. This unique institution not only entertains the public with world-class performances but also plays a critical role in preserving the traditional circus arts and utilizing them as a tool for community engagement and education.

Location/Address and Accessibility

The Circus Arts Conservatory is located at 2075 Bahia Vista Street, Sarasota, Florida. This central location is easily accessible by car from downtown Sarasota and is just a short drive from major highways, making it convenient for both local and visiting patrons. If you're relying on public transportation, several bus routes serve the area, facilitating easy access to the conservatory.

Educational Programs

Education forms the cornerstone of the Conservatory's mission. The organization offers a wide range of educational programs aimed at different age groups, including circus arts classes for youth, where students learn a variety of skills such as juggling, high wire, and acrobatics. These programs are designed not only to preserve circus skills but also to build confidence, improve coordination, and encourage teamwork among participants.

Also, the CAC operates an outreach program called Circus Science, which teaches students the physics behind the circus acts. This program helps to demystify the seemingly magical feats performed in the circus by explaining the scientific principles that make them possible. The Circus Arts Conservatory also hosts lectures and workshops for educators and the general public to further disseminate knowledge about the cultural and historical importance of circus arts.

Performance Aspects

The Circus Arts Conservatory is renowned for its breathtaking performances, which include seasonal shows such as Circus Sarasota and Cirque des Voix®. Circus Sarasota showcases traditional circus artistry, with performances from both internationally renowned artists and the conservatory's students. Cirque des Voix® is a unique production that combines the thrill of circus arts with the power of a live choir and orchestra, providing a truly immersive experience for the audience.

These performances not only highlight the skills and talents of a diverse group of performers but also serve to promote and preserve the circus tradition in Sarasota. The CAC's Big Top performances are particularly popular, drawing large crowds and serving as a key cultural event in the community calendar.

Community Engagement

The Circus Arts Conservatory actively engages with the Sarasota community through various initiatives. One of its flagship community outreach programs is Laughter Unlimited, which uses circus arts to improve the quality of life for seniors in assisted living facilities and nursing homes. This program highlights the therapeutic benefits of laughter and entertainment for emotional and physical health.

Moreover, the CAC provides support and expertise for local events and festivals, helping to enhance the cultural landscape of Sarasota. The conservatory's artists often participate in community parades and public celebrations, adding a touch of spectacle and festivity to these events.

Shopping and Dining

St. Armands Circle

St. Armands Circle stands as a premier shopping and dining destination in Sarasota, offering an elegant blend of past and present with its sophisticated array of boutiques, gourmet restaurants, and lively atmosphere. This renowned commercial hub is not only a focal point for luxury shopping but also a vibrant venue for social gatherings and community events, making it a central component of Sarasota's social and cultural scene.

Location/Address and Accessibility

St. Armands Circle is located at 300 Madison Drive, Sarasota, Florida. Situated on Lido Key, just a bridge away from downtown Sarasota, it is conveniently accessible by car. From downtown, take John Ringling Blvd, which directly leads to the Circle. If you're without a vehicle, Sarasota's public bus service offers routes that connect the mainland to Lido Key, making stops near the Circle.

Unique Shopping Experience

St. Armands Circle is famed for its sophisticated shopping experience, featuring more than 130 stores ranging from high-end fashion boutiques to artisan galleries. The Circle's layout, characterized by its unique circular design and tropical setting, creates an inviting atmosphere for leisurely shopping. Upscale boutiques offer exclusive fashions, jewelry, and accessories, catering to discerning shoppers looking for unique and high-quality items.

Art lovers and collectors will appreciate the fine art galleries that display works by both local and international artists. From sculpture and painting to glasswork and pottery, the range of art available at St. Armands Circle is extensive and diverse.

Dining Options

The dining scene at St. Armands Circle is as diverse as its shopping. The area boasts an impressive array of eateries, ranging from casual cafes to gourmet restaurants. Seafood lovers can indulge in freshly caught fare, while those with a taste for international flavors will find everything from French bistros to Italian trattorias.

Many restaurants offer outdoor seating, which allows diners to enjoy the pleasant Sarasota weather and vibrant street scenes. The combination of fine food, excellent service, and a beautiful atmosphere makes dining out at St. Armands Circle a memorable experience.

Festive Atmosphere

St. Armands Circle is known for its festive atmosphere, enhanced by frequent community events and live entertainment. Throughout the year, the Circle hosts various events such as art festivals, car shows, and holiday-themed festivities, which draw both locals and tourists. The Circle's central park often features live music and performances, adding to the lively ambiance that defines St. Armands.

The landscape is adorned with lush tropical plantings and elegant statues, remnants of John Ringling's vision to create a European-style shopping district. These artistic and botanical elements contribute to the overall charm and appeal of the area, making it not just a shopping destination but a cultural experience.

Sarasota Farmers Market

The Sarasota Farmers Market is a vibrant hub of activity that enriches Sarasota's community life every Saturday morning. Founded in 1979, the market has grown to become more than just a place to buy fresh local produce; it's a weekly event where families, food lovers, and tourists gather to enjoy the bounty and creativity of the region.

Location/Address and How to Get There

The Sarasota Farmers Market is centrally located in downtown Sarasota, spanning Lemon Avenue, Main Street, and State Street. The main intersection is at Lemon Avenue and Main Street. If you're coming from outside Sarasota, you can easily reach the market by driving toward downtown Sarasota. Head to south on I-75, take exit 210 for Fruitville

Road, drive west towards the coast, and follow signs to downtown Sarasota. Parking is available in several public parking lots and garages around the downtown area. Additionally, Sarasota's public transportation services offer routes that stop near the market, making it accessible for everyone without a car.

Offerings at the Market

The Sarasota Farmers Market features a rich assortment of vendors offering everything from fresh fruits and vegetables to prepared foods, artisan crafts, and more. Local farmers display their seasonal produce, providing a colorful array of organic and conventionally grown fruits and vegetables that highlight the region's agricultural diversity. This not only allows consumers to buy directly from the source but also supports the local farming community.

Apart from produce, the market is a foodie's delight with numerous food vendors selling a variety of ready-to-eat meals and snacks. From freshly baked pastries and gourmet cheeses to ethnic cuisines and vegan dishes, there is something to satisfy every palate.

Crafts and Artisan Goods

In addition to food products, the Sarasota Farmers Market serves as a showcase for local artisans and crafters. Vendors offer a wide range of products including handmade jewelry, pottery, artwork, and home décor items. This aspect of the market is particularly important as it provides local artists and craftspeople a venue to reach a broad audience, fostering local talent and entrepreneurship.

Community Role

Beyond being a shopping destination, the Sarasota Farmers Market plays a significant role in community engagement. The market hosts events, live music, and activities that turn shopping into a lively communal activity. It serves as a meeting place where residents and visitors alike can mingle, chat, and enjoy the vibrant atmosphere.

Educational outreach is also a key component of the market's activities. Regular cooking demonstrations, gardening tips, and sustainability workshops educate the public on healthy eating, local farming, and environmentally friendly practices.

The Mall at University Town Center

The Mall at University Town Center (UTC) stands as a premier shopping destination in Sarasota, Florida, offering an expansive array of retail options and dining experiences. Since its opening in October 2014, the Mall has become a central hub for both local shoppers and tourists seeking a high-end shopping experience in the region.

Location/Address and How to Get There

The Mall at University Town Center is located at 140 University Town Center Drive in Sarasota. It is conveniently positioned near the intersection of I-75 and University Parkway, making it easily accessible by car. If you're coming from downtown Sarasota, it is a straightforward drive east on Fruitville Road, turning north onto Cattlemen Road, and then east on University Parkway. The Mall is directly accessible from the interstate, making it a convenient destination for visitors from neighboring cities. There are ample parking facilities available on-site, including multi-level parking garages and surface lots.

Retail Offerings

The Mall at University Town Center spans over 880,000 square feet and features more than 150 stores. It boasts a mix of high-end retailers and mainstream brands, catering to a wide range of tastes and budgets. Shoppers can explore luxury boutiques such as Tesla, Michael Kors, and Apple, alongside popular department stores like Macy's and Dillard's. This variety ensures that the Mall at UTC can offer something for everyone, from the latest fashion and technology to homeware and beauty products.

In addition to the comprehensive range of retail stores, the Mall at UTC is also home to several specialty shops that offer unique products and services. These include art galleries, custom jewelry stores, and high-end cosmetic shops, adding to the Mall's appeal as a shopping haven.

Dining Options

Dining at the Mall at University Town Center is as diverse and satisfying as its shopping. The Mall houses a variety of dining options, from fast casual to upscale restaurants. You can enjoy a quick bite at one of the many fast-food outlets or sit down for a relaxed meal at fine dining establishments. The cuisine options are vast, including American, Italian, Asian, and seafood, ensuring that there are choices to suit every palate.

The Mall also features several cafes and dessert shops, perfect to indulge in a sweet treat or a coffee break during your shopping journey. The presence of these dining options enhances the overall shopping experience, allowing you to spend longer periods at the mall without needing to leave for meals.

Community and Economic Impact

The Mall at University Town Center significantly contributes to the local economy by attracting thousands of visitors each week, which supports employment and generates considerable sales tax revenue. The Mall is not only a shopping destination but also a venue for community events, fashion shows, and public holiday celebrations, which foster community engagement and enhance its role as a social hub in the region.

Moreover, the Mall's management actively participates in community development efforts, partnering with local charities and organizations to host events and fundraisers that support various causes within Sarasota and the surrounding areas.

Chapter 4: Things to Do in Sarasota

Dolphin and Sunset Cruises

Sarasota, Florida, renowned for its sparkling Gulf waters and vibrant bay area, offers an enchanting array of dolphin and sunset cruises that captivate with scenic views and marine wildlife encounters. These cruises provide an unforgettable experience, combining the natural beauty of Sarasota Bay and the Gulf of Mexico with the joy of dolphin watching and the serenity of ocean sunsets.

Scenic Beauty of Sarasota Bay and the Gulf of Mexico

Sarasota Bay, a haven for biodiversity, and the expansive Gulf of Mexico are prime locations for exploring Florida's coastal allure. The area's unique geographical features create an ideal habitat for a variety of marine life, including the friendly and playful dolphins that are often the highlight of any marine tour. The calm and clear waters of the Gulf provide perfect conditions for these majestic creatures to thrive, making dolphin sightings a common delight for cruise participants.

Dolphin Watching

Dolphin cruises in Sarasota are specifically designed to bring you into proximity with these intelligent marine mammals. Experienced captains navigate the waters with a deep understanding of dolphin behaviors and their common habitats. Tour guides provide commentary on the life and habits of dolphins, enhancing the educational value of each excursion. Guests aboard these cruises are often treated to dolphins playfully racing alongside the boat or performing acrobatic jumps, offering spectacular photo opportunities and memorable encounters.

Sunset Cruises

As the day winds down, sunset cruises take center stage, offering a romantic and awe-inspiring vista of the sun dipping below the horizon. These cruises are particularly popular among couples and photography enthusiasts eager to capture the sky painted in vibrant hues of orange, pink, and purple. The tranquil waters reflect the sunset, creating a stunning tableau that embodies peace and natural beauty.

Combination Tours

Many operators in Sarasota offer cruises that combine dolphin watching with sunset views, providing a comprehensive sea experience. These tours typically begin in the late afternoon, allowing guests to enjoy the warmth of the sun before transitioning to the cooler, picturesque evening skies. Onboard amenities often include refreshments or a champagne toast, adding an extra touch of luxury to the journey.

Choosing the Right Cruise

Several reputable companies offer dolphin and sunset cruises from various points along Sarasota's coast. Selections range from large, comfortable boats with ample seating to more intimate sailing experiences. Depending on the time of year and weather conditions, different cruise options can provide varying experiences, from serene, smooth sailing to more adventurous, wind-driven routes.

Engagement with Nature and Conservation

Participating in a dolphin and sunset cruise in Sarasota not only entertains but also educates guests about marine conservation and the importance of protecting natural habitats. Many tour operators emphasize eco-friendly practices and educate passengers on how to observe wildlife responsibly. This commitment to conservation helps ensure that the beauty and diversity of Sarasota's marine environments remain intact for future generations.

Kayaking and Paddleboarding Adventures

Sarasota, Florida, offers a wealth of natural waterways, making it an ideal destination for kayaking and paddleboarding enthusiasts. From the serene waters of Lido Key to the mysterious mangrove tunnels near Siesta Key, the region is dotted with superb locations that provide both recreational and exploratory opportunities for paddlers of all skill levels.

Lido Key

Lido Key is renowned for its calm, clear waters, which are perfect for paddleboarding. The area offers expansive views of Sarasota Bay and the Gulf of Mexico, and its gentle currents make it an excellent spot for beginners. You can explore the key's intricate coastline and may even encounter local wildlife, such as dolphins and manatees, which are frequent visitors to these waters.

Mangrove Tunnels Near Siesta Key

The mangrove tunnels near Siesta Key are a must-visit for kayaking enthusiasts. This natural network of shaded waterways offers a unique paddling experience as you navigate through tight spaces surrounded by lush greenery. The tunnels provide a habitat for a variety of wildlife, including fish, birds, and the occasional raccoon or otter. This area not only challenges your paddling skills but also offers an up-close look at Florida's rich ecological system.

Other Popular Spots for Kayaking and Paddleboarding

- Myakka River State Park: This park is one of Florida's largest and oldest state parks where the Myakka River flows through 58 square miles of wetlands, prairies, hammocks, and pinelands. Paddlers can explore the scenic river and two lakes, encountering abundant wildlife and enjoying fishing spots along the way.
- South Lido Nature Park: Located at the southern tip of Lido Key, this park includes a paddle trail that winds through a mesmerizing mangrove forest. The calm and shallow waters here are ideal for paddleboarding, offering a peaceful retreat with spectacular views of Sarasota's skyline.
- Nathan Benderson Park: This park features a man-made lake that hosts international rowing events and is also open for public kayaking and paddleboarding. Its controlled environment makes it safe for beginners and families.
- Sarasota Bay: This large body of water offers more open and challenging conditions for experienced kayakers and paddleboarders. It is perfect to combine a workout with spectacular views of the coast.

- Blackburn Point: Located on the Intracoastal Waterway, this area offers diverse water conditions and scenery that change with the tides. It's ideal for more adventurous paddlers looking to explore different ecosystems and water environments.

Environmental and Safety Considerations

While embarking on kayaking and paddleboarding adventures, it is crucial to consider environmental conservation and safety. Paddlers should be mindful of the wildlife and habitats they encounter, avoiding areas that are restricted for conservation efforts. It is also important to wear life jackets, check weather conditions, and use suitable equipment for the water conditions.

Fishing Charters

For enthusiasts of the rod and reel, Sarasota, Florida, presents a paradise teeming with deep-sea and inshore fishing opportunities. The city's proximity to the Gulf of Mexico opens up a vast aquatic playground where anglers can engage in some of the most exhilarating fishing experiences, targeting a diverse array of game fish that inhabit these waters.

Deep-Sea Fishing Charters

Deep-sea fishing charters in Sarasota are a gateway to the open waters, where the depth and currents bring a chance to catch some of the ocean's most prized species. These charters typically venture into the Gulf of Mexico, reaching depths where grouper, snapper, kingfish, and tarpon thrive. If you're seeking a truly challenging experience, some charters offer the opportunity to wrestle with the mighty sailfish or marlin.

The boats used for these expeditions are equipped with the latest fishing technology and gear, ensuring that even the most seasoned anglers have the tools they need to make a great catch. Skilled captains navigate these waters with expertise, relying on years of local fishing knowledge and understanding of marine weather patterns to provide a safe and productive outing.

Variety of Species in Local Waters

Sarasota's waters are rich in biodiversity, making them an ideal spot for both amateur and professional anglers. In addition to the deep-sea giants, the area is home to a variety of other species, including:

- Redfish: Known for their resilience and strength, redfish are a popular target in Sarasota's shallower waters.
- Snook: These fish are known for their powerful runs and are a favorite among sport fishing enthusiasts.
- Spotted Seatrout: Often found in the grassy flats, these fish provide good sport due to their aggressive feeding habits.
- Sheepshead: Recognizable by their distinctive black and white stripes, sheepshead are often found around piers and jetties, making them a fun challenge for anglers of all levels.

Fishing Tournaments and Events

Sarasota hosts several fishing tournaments throughout the year, which draw competitors from across the nation. These events often focus on specific species, such as tarpon, and offer anglers a chance to showcase their skills in a competitive setting. Participation in these tournaments not only provides an exciting challenge but also promotes camaraderie and community among fishing enthusiasts.

Sustainable Fishing Practices

Recognizing the need to preserve its marine ecosystems, many Sarasota fishing charters advocate for and practice sustainable fishing methods. Catch-and-release policies are common, especially for species like tarpon, which are sought after for sport rather than food. Charters also adhere to all local regulations regarding size and bag limits to ensure that fish populations remain healthy for future generations.

Golfing in Sarasota

Sarasota, Florida, is a golfer's paradise, boasting a variety of golf courses known for their challenging layouts and stunning environments. These courses cater to all skill levels, from novices to professional players, and provide an excellent blend of natural beauty and sporting challenges. Here's a look at some of Sarasota's premier golfing destinations, each offering unique features that make the most of the region's picturesque landscapes and pleasant climate.

TPC Prestancia

Located in the heart of Sarasota, TPC Prestancia is part of the prestigious Tournament Players Club network and offers two 18-hole championship courses: the Stadium Course and the Club Course. Both courses are known for their meticulous landscaping and challenging holes. The Stadium Course, in particular, features undulating greens and strategic water hazards that test even the most skilled golfers. TPC Prestancia is also a certified Audubon Cooperative Sanctuary, highlighting its commitment to maintaining the natural environment.

The Concession Golf Club

This course is renowned for its challenging layout and impeccable design, co-designed by Jack Nicklaus and Tony Jacklin. Located on the outskirts of Sarasota, The Concession is named in honor of the famous Ryder Cup moment of sportsmanship between its designers. It features deep bunkers, expansive waste areas, and large, undulating greens, making precision and strategy a necessity for each hole. The natural beauty of the surrounding landscape enhances the secluded feel of the course, making it a luxurious and tranquil golfing experience.

Sarasota National Golf Club

Situated in nearby Venice, Sarasota National offers a pristine golfing experience in an 18-hole championship course that winds through natural wetlands, dense forests, and open vistas. The course is designed to challenge players with water hazards and strategic bunkering while providing breathtaking views and a serene atmosphere. It also includes a large practice facility with a driving range, putting greens, and a short game area to help golfers sharpen their skills.

University Park Country Club

University Park has consistently been rated as one of the best golf courses in the region, offering 27 holes spread across three rotating nines named the Park, River, and University. These courses are known for their scenic beauty, featuring rippling fairways, dense woodland buffers, and natural waterways. The layout demands accuracy and thoughtful play, with each nine offering a different set of challenges and aesthetic appeal.

Bobby Jones Golf Club

This historic public golf facility offers two 18-hole championship courses, the British Course and the American Course, each providing a distinct playing experience. The British Course features wide-open fairways reminiscent of traditional Scottish links, while the American Course presents more tree-lined fairways and requires more precision. Located within the city limits of Sarasota, Bobby Jones Golf Club is an accessible option for both locals and visitors looking to enjoy a round of golf without traveling far.

Golfing Amenities and Services

Most of these golf clubs offer more than just excellent playing conditions; they come equipped with pro shops stocked with the latest gear, practice facilities, and professional instruction to help golfers improve their game. Many clubs also feature luxurious clubhouses where players can relax and dine in comfort, enjoying views of the course with fine dining or casual eating options.

Art Galleries and Studios Hopping

Sarasota, Florida, renowned for its vibrant cultural landscape, boasts a thriving art scene that reflects the city's rich artistic heritage and contemporary creativity. This city is a haven for art lovers, featuring an impressive array of galleries and studios that showcase the works of both local and international artists. From traditional fine art to modern installations and experimental mediums, Sarasota's galleries and studios offer something to intrigue you.

Allyn Gallup Contemporary Art

Located in downtown Sarasota, Allyn Gallup Contemporary Art is known for its curated selection of contemporary artworks. This gallery features a dynamic range of paintings, sculptures, and mixed-media pieces by mid-career and established artists. Exhibitions here often explore compelling themes and present innovative perspectives that will challenge and delight you.

Art Uptown Gallery

As Sarasota's oldest fine arts gallery, Art Uptown Gallery represents a diverse group of local artists. Situated on Main Street, the gallery displays a wide array of artistic styles and mediums, including painting, photography, sculpture, and jewelry. Art Uptown is unique in that it is managed and staffed by the artists themselves, offering personal insight into the art on display and the opportunity to meet the creators during gallery visits.

Selby Gallery at Ringling College of Art and Design

The Selby Gallery, located on the campus of the prestigious Ringling College of Art and Design, serves as a critical space for contemporary art in Sarasota. It hosts exhibitions from internationally recognized artists, designers, and scholars, along with showcasing the work of the college's students and faculty. The gallery not only features visual arts but also includes lectures, panel discussions, and community workshops that foster a deeper understanding of the arts.

Towles Court Artist Colony

If you're interested in a more immersive artistic experience, the Towles Court Artist Colony offers a unique setting. This artist-run neighborhood features colorful bungalows that house studios and galleries. You can stroll through the leafy paths, explore the open studios, and interact with artists at work. On the third Friday of each month, Towles Court hosts an art walk, featuring live music and a festive atmosphere that celebrates the local art community.

State of the Arts Gallery

State of the Arts Gallery is renowned for showcasing cutting-edge contemporary art. The gallery emphasizes fine art created by Sarasota's leading artists and often introduces exciting new talents from around the world. Their offerings are diverse, ranging from abstract expressionism to realistic portraiture, making it a key destination for collectors and art enthusiasts alike.

Clyde Butcher's St. Armands Gallery

Famed photographer Clyde Butcher, known for his stunning black-and-white landscape photography, has a gallery in St. Armands Circle. His dramatic, large-format photographs capture the beauty of Florida's wilderness areas, particularly the Everglades. The gallery not only displays Butcher's works but also hosts photography workshops and eco-tours, offering a unique blend of art and environmental education.

Palm Avenue Fine Art

Located on the fashionable Palm Avenue, this gallery specializes in representational art, featuring works by nationally and internationally acclaimed artists. Palm Avenue Fine Art offers a classic gallery experience with a focus on high-quality paintings and sculptures that celebrate Florida's scenic beauty and cultural heritage.

Tasting Local Craft Breweries and Wineries

Sarasota, Florida, has developed a vibrant craft beer and wine scene, appealing to aficionados and casual tasters alike. The region's warm climate and creative culture have fostered a community of breweries and wineries known for their innovative and flavorful beverages. Here's a deeper dive into the local craft beer and wine scene, highlighting some must-visit spots.

Craft Breweries in Sarasota

Big Top Brewing Company

Big Top Brewing Company captures the spirit of Sarasota's circus heritage with its circus-themed beers and taproom. Known for crafting unique flavors, some of their popular offerings include the Circus City IPA and the Trapeze Monk Belgian Style Wit. You can enjoy a relaxed atmosphere with a food menu that complements their brews perfectly.

Calusa Brewing

Focused on producing bold, inspired craft beers, Calusa Brewing has quickly established itself as a cornerstone of Sarasota's craft beer scene. Their emphasis is on aromatic, hop-forward ales and complex, barrel-aged strong beers. The taproom offers an ever-changing lineup of brews, ensuring there is always something new to taste.

JDub's Brewing Company

JDub's Brewing Company offers a range of beers from flagship brews to innovative experimental ales. Located near downtown Sarasota, JDub's features a taproom and a beer garden where they host live music and food trucks, making it a perfect spot for an evening out.

Motorworks Brewing

Originally based in Bradenton, Motorworks Brewing features a Sarasota taproom with a broad selection of beers, from traditional lagers to inventive IPAs. The venue is known for its vibrant atmosphere and often hosts events and live performances, which make it a popular gathering spot.

Local Wineries

Fiorelli Winery

Located just east of Sarasota in Bradenton, Fiorelli Winery is one of the few vineyards in the region. They offer a range of estate-grown wines that reflect the terroir of the area. The winery provides tours and tastings, where guests can learn about the winemaking process and sample a variety of wines.

Bunker Hill Vineyard and Winery

A short drive from Sarasota, Bunker Hill Vineyard and Winery is known for its environmentally friendly practices and 100% recyclable wines. The winery offers a unique lineup of wines made from locally sourced fruits and traditional wine grapes, all available for tasting in their green-certified tasting room.

Wine Bars and Tastings

Michael's On East

While not a winery, Michael's On East is an award-winning restaurant in Sarasota that features an impressive wine cellar. They offer wine tastings and pairings, which are guided by knowledgeable staff, making it a great place to learn more about wines from around the world.

Sarasota Wine Club

If you're looking to deepen your knowledge of wines, the Sarasota Wine Club offers monthly tasting events where members can sample and learn about a variety of wines, focusing on different regions and themes each month.

Shopping at UTC Mall

The Mall at University Town Center (UTC Mall) stands as a beacon of modern retail and dining in Sarasota, Florida. Opened in October 2014, this premier shopping destination draws both locals and tourists with its wide array of offerings, including high-end boutiques, large department stores, and a diverse selection of eateries. Its sophisticated design and vibrant atmosphere make it more than just a shopping center—it's a central gathering place for the community.

Location and Accessibility

The Mall at University Town Center is located at 140 University Town Center Drive, Sarasota, Florida. Strategically situated at the intersection of I-75 and University Parkway, it is easily accessible from anywhere in the region. This prime location near the interstate allows for straightforward access if you're coming from the neighboring cities and counties.

To get there by car from downtown Sarasota, take Fruitville Road east to Cattlemen Road, then head north until reaching University Parkway, where you turn east. The mall is just a few minutes down the road, with clear signs leading to ample parking, which includes multi-story garages and surface lots.

Public transportation is also an option, with several bus routes servicing the area, ensuring convenient access if you prefer not to drive.

Retail Offerings

UTC Mall spans over two floors and features more than 150 stores, appealing to a wide range of tastes and budgets. Shoppers can explore luxury brands like Michael Kors, Kate Spade, and Tesla, as well as popular high-street retailers such as Apple, Anthropologie, and Lululemon. Major department stores include Macy's, Dillard's, and Saks Fifth Avenue, providing a comprehensive shopping experience that caters to all needs—from fashion and beauty products to technology and home goods.

The mall also hosts several specialty shops that offer unique products and services, ranging from high-end jewelry to bespoke tailoring and spa treatments, ensuring a full-service shopping experience.

Dining Options

The Mall at University Town Center isn't just about shopping; it also offers a diverse culinary landscape. The dining options range from fast casual to gourmet restaurants, with flavors from around the globe. Patrons can enjoy meals at upscale restaurants like The Capital Grille and Seasons 52, or grab a quick bite at Cheesecake Factory or Brio Tuscan Grille. If you're looking for a more relaxed vibe, there are numerous cafes and eateries scattered throughout the mall, providing perfect spots to recharge between shopping sessions.

In addition to sit-down dining, the mall features several food courts and snack kiosks, offering everything from coffee and pastries to ice cream and pretzels, catering to all tastes and dietary preferences.

Community and Events

UTC Mall is more than a shopping destination; it's a vibrant center of activity in Sarasota. The mall frequently hosts community events, including fashion shows, holiday celebrations, and charity events, which contribute to its role as a community hub. These events are well-attended and add an extra layer of engagement to the shopping experience, enhancing the mall's appeal as a place to shop, dine, and gather.

Chapter 5: Where To Stay

Luxury Hotels and Resorts

The Resort at Longboat Key Club

The Resort at Longboat Key Club stands as a distinguished and serene oasis along the Gulf of Mexico, offering an extensive array of leisure and luxury amenities. Situated on a barrier island off the coast of Sarasota, this upscale resort is designed for an exquisite vacation experience, combining natural beauty with refined luxury.

Location/Address

The Resort at Longboat Key Club is located at 220 Sands Point Road, Longboat Key, Florida. This exclusive resort is set on a stunning stretch of sandy beach, offering breathtaking views and a tranquil atmosphere that defines coastal luxury.

Getting There

Accessing the Resort at Longboat Key Club is straightforward whether you are arriving from nearby or traveling from afar. If you're flying in, the closest major airport is Sarasota-Bradenton International Airport, which is approximately a 20-minute drive from the resort. From the airport, you can take US-41 south to Gulfstream Avenue, then follow it onto John Ringling Causeway and continue to Gulf of Mexico Drive, which leads directly to Longboat Key. The resort is well-signposted along this scenic route.

If you're driving from Tampa, the drive takes about an hour and a half via I-75 S, exiting onto University Parkway westbound, which eventually merges with Gulf of Mexico Drive. The scenic drive along the coast sets the stage for the calming retreat that awaits at the resort.

Key Amenities

- Golf Courses: The resort boasts two championship golf courses that cater to golf enthusiasts looking to play amidst meticulously landscaped greens and sweeping views.

- Tennis Gardens: With 20 Har-Tru clay courts, a professional shop, and available instruction, the tennis facilities are ranked among the top in the country.
- Spa and Fitness Center: A full-service spa offers a wide range of treatments designed to rejuvenate and relax, while the state-of-the-art fitness center provides classes and equipment to help guests maintain their wellness routine.
- Dining Options: Multiple dining venues at the resort range from casual beachfront eateries to fine dining establishments, serving a variety of cuisines to suit every palate.
- Marina: The on-site marina offers direct access to the Gulf of Mexico, with boat rentals and fishing charters available for nautical adventures.
- Beach Access: Direct access to a private, white sandy beach provides the perfect setting for sunbathing, swimming, and water sports.

Ideal For
- Family Vacations: With activities and amenities that appeal to all ages, from children's programs to adult-only areas, the resort is an ideal location for families seeking a memorable beach vacation.
- Romantic Getaways: The resort's picturesque setting, combined with luxurious accommodations and private amenities, makes it a prime choice for couples looking for a romantic escape.
- Golf and Tennis Enthusiasts: The professional-grade golf and tennis facilities cater perfectly to sports enthusiasts looking to enjoy premium playing conditions.
- Wellness Seekers: Those focused on health and wellness will find the spa, fitness center, and healthy dining options align well with a rejuvenating holiday theme.

The Resort at Longboat Key Club excels in providing a luxurious and comprehensive vacation experience. Its combination of natural beauty, exceptional facilities, and attentive service ensures that you will find something to love, making it a standout destination in the Sarasota area.

The Ritz-Carlton, Sarasota

The Ritz-Carlton, Sarasota, represents the pinnacle of luxury and elegance in one of Florida's most culturally vibrant and beautiful cities.

This hotel not only captures the essence of Sarasota's sophisticated style but also provides an array of top-tier amenities, making it a preferred destination for both leisure and business travelers.

Location/Address

The Ritz-Carlton, Sarasota is located at 1111 Ritz-Carlton Drive, Sarasota, Florida. Nestled along the Gulf Coast, this prime location offers stunning views of Sarasota Bay and is conveniently situated near downtown Sarasota's array of shops, restaurants, and entertainment options.

Getting There

The hotel is accessible via several major routes. If you're arriving from Sarasota-Bradenton International Airport can reach the hotel in about 15 minutes by car, primarily via US-41 (Tamiami Trail) heading south, making it a convenient option for both domestic and international travelers. If you're driving from cities like Tampa or St. Petersburg, I-75 is the most direct route, connecting to FL-780 W (Fruitville Road) which leads directly to downtown Sarasota.

Key Amenities

- The Ritz-Carlton, Sarasota is renowned for its wide range of luxurious amenities, designed to cater to every aspect of guest comfort and convenience:
- Spa and Wellness: The hotel features a full-service spa offering a variety of treatments, massages, and wellness programs tailored to rejuvenate and relax the body and mind.
- Golf and Sports: Guests have access to an exclusive golf club located just a short drive from the hotel, featuring an 18-hole championship course set in a beautiful landscape.
- Dining: The Ritz-Carlton offers several dining options, including a waterfront restaurant that serves fresh seafood and a farm-to-table menu that highlights local ingredients.
- Fitness Center and Pools: A state-of-the-art fitness center and a beautifully designed outdoor pool area provide guests with ample opportunities for exercise and leisure.

- Event Spaces: The hotel boasts extensive meeting and event spaces, making it an ideal venue for conferences, weddings, and other large gatherings.

Ideal For
Luxury Travelers: With its sumptuous accommodations and first-rate amenities, The Ritz-Carlton is perfect for a luxurious getaway.

- Business Professionals: The hotel's comprehensive business facilities, including high-tech meeting rooms and business services, cater to the needs of business travelers.
- Couples and Families: The range of amenities from the spa to the children's programs ensures that both couples and families will find activities and services tailored to their needs.
- Golf Enthusiasts: Access to a top-tier golf course is a major draw for guests who enjoy spending time on the links.

The Ritz-Carlton, Sarasota is more than just a hotel—it is a destination that offers a refined experience combining relaxation, luxury, and access to the best of Sarasota.

Zota Beach Resort
Nestled along the pristine shores of Longboat Key, Zota Beach Resort offers a luxurious and tranquil retreat in one of Florida's most picturesque coastal areas. This upscale resort combines modern style and amenities with easy access to the natural beauty and recreational activities of the Gulf Coast.

Location/Address
Zota Beach Resort is located at 4711 Gulf of Mexico Drive, Longboat Key, Florida. This idyllic setting is situated on a stretch of private beach, providing guests with exclusive access to one of the area's most beautiful coastlines.

Getting There
The resort is conveniently accessible for both local and international travelers. If you're flying in, the closest major airport is Sarasota-Bradenton International Airport, which is about a 20-minute drive from the resort. To reach Zota Beach Resort from the airport, take University

Parkway west from the airport exit, then turn south onto US-41/Tamiami Trail. Continue to Gulfstream Avenue, which leads over the John Ringling Causeway onto Longboat Key. Once on the island, proceed north on the Gulf of Mexico Drive to the resort.

Guests driving from Tampa or St. Petersburg can expect a scenic drive of approximately one to one and a half hours via I-75 S, taking the exit for University Parkway westbound, and following the same route across the causeway onto Longboat Key.

Key Amenities
- Private Beach Access: You can enjoy a secluded and beautiful beach right on the Gulf of Mexico, perfect for sunbathing, swimming, and sunset viewing.
- Modern Accommodations: The resort offers stylish rooms and suites with private balconies, many of which provide stunning views of the Gulf.
- Outdoor Pool and Sun Deck: A spacious outdoor pool area allows guests to relax and soak up the Florida sun, with a poolside bar serving refreshing drinks and light meals.
- Fitness Center: A fully equipped fitness center is available to guests who wish to maintain their workout routine while on vacation.
- Dining Options: Zota Beach Resort features an on-site restaurant that specializes in fresh seafood and local cuisine, alongside a wine bar offering a selection of fine wines and spirits.
- Event Spaces: With versatile indoor and outdoor venues, the resort is an ideal location for weddings, corporate events, and private parties.

Ideal For
- Couples and Romantic Getaways: The resort's serene beach, luxurious accommodations, and fine dining options make it a perfect destination for couples looking for a romantic escape.
- Families: With family-friendly amenities and activities, parents and children alike will find plenty to enjoy during their stay.
- Wellness Enthusiasts: The fitness center and wellness-focused amenities cater to guests who prioritize health and relaxation.

- Business Travelers and Event Planners: State-of-the-art facilities and beautiful settings provide the perfect backdrop for corporate retreats and conferences.

Zota Beach Resort exemplifies the best of Longboat Key's luxury accommodations, offering a blend of relaxation, style, and convenience.

Hyatt Regency Sarasota

Located in the vibrant heart of Sarasota, Florida, the Hyatt Regency Sarasota offers a luxurious waterfront escape that embodies the essence of coastal elegance combined with modern amenities. This prime location not only provides stunning views of Sarasota Bay but also places guests within easy reach of the city's most notable attractions, including museums, theaters, and the bustling downtown area.

Location/Address

The Hyatt Regency Sarasota is situated at 1000 Boulevard of the Arts, Sarasota, Florida, 34236. This address places the hotel right in the cultural and scenic hub of Sarasota, with direct access to the bay and marina.

Getting There

If you're arriving by air, the Sarasota-Bradenton International Airport is conveniently located just about 4 miles north of the hotel, making it a quick 10-minute drive. You should take University Parkway west from the airport, turn left onto US-41 South/Tamiami Trail, and then turn right onto Boulevard of the Arts. Zota Beach Resort will be on the left.

Suppose you're driving from nearby cities like Tampa or St. Petersburg. In that case, you can reach the hotel via I-75 S, taking exit 213 to University Parkway, proceeding west, and following the same directions from US-41 South to the hotel.

Key Amenities

- Marina Access: Guests can enjoy the scenic marina with boat docks and charters available for sailing, fishing, or cruising around Sarasota Bay.

- Lagoon-Style Pool: The hotel features a stunning 130-foot lagoon-style outdoor pool, complete with a cascading waterfall and a sundeck that offers panoramic views of the bay and marina.
- Fitness Center: A state-of-the-art fitness center equipped with the latest exercise machines and a variety of fitness classes to keep guests active and energized.
- Dining Options: The hotel boasts several dining venues, including a waterfront restaurant that serves fresh seafood and local cuisine, providing a perfect setting for a romantic dinner or a casual meal with views of the sunset over the bay.
- Spa Services: On-site spa services are available, offering a range of treatments designed to pamper guests and provide a relaxing retreat from the hustle and bustle of daily life.
- Event and Conference Facilities: With over 20,000 square feet of flexible meeting space, including a grand ballroom and multiple smaller venues, the hotel is an ideal location for conferences, weddings, and other large gatherings.

Ideal For

- Business Travelers: With extensive conference facilities and a prime location near downtown Sarasota, the Hyatt Regency is ideal for professionals seeking a convenient and upscale venue for business engagements.
- Couples: The hotel's romantic waterfront setting and luxurious amenities offer couples a perfect getaway destination.
- Families: Family-friendly amenities, including the pool, nearby beaches, and available family rooms, make the hotel suitable for guests traveling with children.
- Wellness Seekers: Those looking to relax and rejuvenate will find the hotel's spa services and tranquil environment ideal for a wellness-focused vacation.

The Hyatt Regency Sarasota provides an exemplary model of how a hotel can offer luxury, comfort, and convenience in one package. Its commitment to quality service, attention to detail in guest experiences, and prime location make it a standout choice for anyone visiting Sarasota.

The Westin Sarasota

Nestled gracefully in the vibrant heart of Sarasota, The Westin Sarasota emerges as a beacon of luxury and tranquility. With its strategic location and comprehensive array of amenities, the hotel invites both leisure and business travelers to indulge in an experience where every stay is crafted to revitalize the spirit and invigorate the senses.

Location and Address

The Westin Sarasota is located at 1175 North Gulfstream Avenue, Sarasota, Florida, 34236. Positioned in the bustling downtown district, this address places guests at the epicenter of cultural richness—surrounded by art galleries, theaters, and a plethora of dining options, encapsulating the vibrant lifestyle of Sarasota.

Directions to the Hotel

Getting to The Westin Sarasota is seamless from any direction. Those arriving from Sarasota-Bradenton International Airport will find it a convenient 10-minute drive by heading south on US-41, a major thoroughfare that threads through the city. If you're coming from Tampa, a 60-minute drive on I-75 south to exit 210 for Fruitville Road, which leads directly into downtown Sarasota, proves a swift route. The proximity to major roads and highways ensures that access is hassle-free, whether by car, taxi, or public transportation.

Key Amenities

The Westin Sarasota distinguishes itself with an array of exceptional amenities designed to enhance every aspect of a guest's stay:

- Heavenly Bed and Bath: Guests can luxuriate in the renowned Westin Heavenly Bed, providing unmatched comfort and restfulness, accompanied by spa-like bathroom amenities for a rejuvenating experience.
- Rooftop Pool and Lounge: The jewel in the crown is the rooftop pool that offers panoramic views of Sarasota Bay, complemented by a chic lounge area—a perfect backdrop for evening cocktails or a serene afternoon soak.
- State-of-the-Art Fitness Studio: With 24/7 access to its world-class WestinWORKOUT Fitness Studio, guests can keep up with their

fitness regime while on the road, equipped with modern machinery and various fitness classes.

- Elevated Dining: The hotel boasts multiple dining venues, including a signature restaurant that melds local flavors with gourmet innovation, and a stylish bar offering creative mixology and fine wines.
- Spa and Wellness Programs: Embrace wellness with Westin's in-house spa services, offering a comprehensive menu of massages, body treatments, and beauty services, ensuring guests leave feeling better than when they arrived.
- Versatile Event Spaces: If you're seeking a venue for weddings, meetings, or any large gathering, The Westin Sarasota offers versatile event spaces with state-of-the-art facilities and breathtaking views, managed by a team of professionals to ensure seamless execution.

Ideal For

- Business Travelers: The Westin Sarasota caters excellently to business professionals with its sophisticated meeting spaces, high-speed internet, and a central location near corporate hubs.
- Couples and Romantics: Its stunning views, luxurious accommodations, and fine dining make it a prime choice for couples seeking a romantic getaway.
- Families: Family-friendly amenities, including spacious rooms and children's programs, make it ideal for guests traveling with children.
- Wellness Seekers: With its focus on rejuvenating spa treatments and a dedicated wellness program, the hotel is a sanctuary to unwind and relax.

Boutiques and Bed & Breakfast

Art Ovation Hotel, Autograph Collection

Nestled in the cultural heart of downtown Sarasota, the Art Ovation Hotel stands out as a vibrant hub of artistic expression and refined hospitality, part of Marriott's prestigious Autograph Collection. This unique property not only offers luxury accommodations but also immerses guests in the local arts scene, making it an exceptional destination for culturally inclined travelers and creative minds.

Location and Address
Art Ovation Hotel is centrally located at 1255 North Palm Avenue, Sarasota, Florida. This prime location places it within walking distance of Sarasota's most famous theaters, galleries, and museums, as well as the bustling downtown area known for its shops, restaurants, and entertainment options.

Getting There
Reaching the Art Ovation Hotel is convenient for both flying visitors and those driving into the city. The nearest airport is Sarasota-Bradenton International Airport, located just about 4 miles north of the hotel, a short 10-minute drive away. You can take a taxi, rideshare, or rental car directly from the airport by heading south on Tamiami Trail (US-41) and turning right onto Fruitville Road, followed by a left onto North Palm Avenue.

If you're driving from nearby cities such as Tampa or St. Petersburg, the drive is straightforward. Take I-75 South to exit 210 for Fruitville Road, head west towards downtown Sarasota, and follow signs to North Palm Avenue.

Key Amenities
- Art Programs and Exhibitions: True to its name, Art Ovation Hotel features rotating art exhibitions throughout the lobby and public spaces, curated by local artists. The hotel offers a schedule of live performances and workshops, where guests can engage directly with the vibrant Sarasota arts community.
- Rooftop Pool and Lounge: Guests can unwind at the rooftop pool and lounge area, which offers spectacular views of the city skyline along with a relaxing atmosphere for sunbathing or enjoying a cocktail.
- Fitness Center and Recreational Activities: A well-equipped fitness center is available for guest use, along with access to recreational activities like golf and tennis at nearby facilities.
- Dining Options: The hotel boasts several dining venues, including Overture Restaurant & Gallery Lounge, which serves a creative menu inspired by local flavors, and Perspective Rooftop Pool Bar, perfect for light meals and evening drinks.

- Luxurious Guest Rooms: Each room and suite is artfully decorated, featuring modern amenities and thoughtful artistic touches. Rooms offer high-speed internet access, luxurious bedding, and state-of-the-art entertainment systems.

Ideal For

- Art Lovers and Creative Individuals: With its focus on art and cultural immersion, the hotel is perfect for guests who appreciate creativity in all its forms.
- Business Travelers: The hotel's central location, business amenities, and meeting spaces make it suitable for professionals looking for a convenient and inspiring environment.
- Leisure Travelers: Those looking to explore Sarasota's rich cultural landscape will find Art Ovation Hotel ideally situated near major attractions and entertainment venues.
- Couples: The hotel's artistic ambiance and luxurious amenities provide a romantic backdrop for a couple's getaway.

The Sarasota Modern, a Tribute Portfolio Hotel

Perched in the vibrant Rosemary District of Sarasota, The Sarasota Modern strives to offer an oasis of style and comfort. As a member of the Tribute Portfolio, this hotel is designed to appeal to those who seek a fusion of classic style and modern amenities within an artistic urban setting.

Location/Address

The Sarasota Modern is located at 1290 Boulevard of the Arts, Sarasota, Florida. This address places it right in the heart of Sarasota's burgeoning arts district, known for its galleries, boutiques, and vibrant street life.

Getting There

Arriving at The Sarasota Modern is hassle-free whether you're coming from near or far. Those flying in will find Sarasota-Bradenton International Airport the most convenient, just a 10-minute drive away. From the airport, you can head south on US-41, turn left onto University Parkway, then right onto Tamiami Trail, and continue until they reach Boulevard of the Arts, where a left turn leads directly to the hotel.

If you're driving from Tampa, the journey typically takes just over an hour via I-75 South. Exiting at University Parkway, westbound leads directly to the arts district, with clear signage directing you to the hotel.

Key Amenities

- Rooftop Pool and Bar: The hotel features a stunning rooftop pool that offers panoramic views of the Sarasota skyline, complete with a chic bar for guests to enjoy bespoke cocktails.
- Fitness Center: A fully-equipped fitness center is available to all guests, featuring a range of modern exercise equipment that caters to all fitness levels.
- Event Spaces: The Sarasota Modern provides elegant spaces for events, including a ballroom and several meeting rooms that blend modern design with functional technology.
- Dining Options: The hotel boasts multiple dining venues, including a signature restaurant that offers an innovative menu inspired by global cuisines with a local twist, and a coffee bar for casual meetups.
- Artistic Decor: Reflecting its location in the Rosemary District, the hotel's interiors are a testament to modern design and local artistry, creating an environment that is both inspiring and relaxing.

Ideal For

- Cultural Enthusiasts: Situated in the arts district, the hotel is perfect for guests eager to explore galleries, theatres, and cultural performances.
- Business Travelers: With state-of-the-art meeting facilities and easy access to downtown Sarasota, business guests will find The Sarasota Modern well-suited for both work and relaxation.
- Leisure Travelers: Those looking for a stylish escape will appreciate the hotel's luxurious amenities, including the pool, spa services, and fine dining.
- Wedding Parties and Special Events: The hotel's modern aesthetic and comprehensive event facilities make it an ideal backdrop for weddings, parties, and other celebrations.

The Sarasota Modern, a Tribute Portfolio Hotel, encapsulates the essence of Sarasota's artistic vibrancy while providing a retreat that speaks to the luxury and comfort expected by today's discerning traveler. With its thoughtful amenities and prime location, it offers a unique stay experience that is both enriching and profoundly enjoyable.

Hotel Indigo - Sarasota

Hotel Indigo Sarasota stands as a vibrant and artful oasis located in the charming coastal town of Sarasota, Florida. This boutique hotel, part of the IHG brand, draws inspiration from its neighborhood to offer a unique, story-rich experience that reflects the culture and atmosphere of its surroundings.

Location/Address

Hotel Indigo is situated at 1223 Boulevard of the Arts, Sarasota, Florida. This location places it within the arts district of Sarasota, making it an ideal spot for guests who are interested in exploring the artistic and cultural offerings of the city.

Getting There

If you're arriving by air you will find the Sarasota-Bradenton International Airport most convenient, located just about 4 miles from the hotel. To reach Hotel Indigo, you can take a short taxi or rideshare journey from the airport by heading south on US-41, turning right on University Parkway, and then making a left on Tamiami Trail until reaching Boulevard of the Arts, where a right turn leads straight to the hotel's doorstep.

If you're driving from Tampa, the journey can be completed in approximately an hour via I-75 South. Take exit 213 for University Parkway, head west toward the bay, and follow signs to downtown Sarasota, turning onto Tamiami Trail and proceeding to Boulevard of the Arts.

Key Amenities

- Pet-Friendly Policy: Hotel Indigo welcomes guests and their pets, offering specific accommodations that cater to pet owners.
- Health and Wellness: A fully equipped fitness center and a whirlpool are available for guest use, ideal for relaxation and maintaining workout routines while away from home.
- Dining: The hotel features the H2O Bistro, which offers a locally sourced menu and specializes in fresh, innovative cuisine. The bistro

provides a casual yet refined dining experience with both indoor and outdoor seating.

- Meeting and Event Space: For business travelers or those hosting events, Hotel Indigo offers flexible meeting spaces equipped with the latest technology, perfect for conferences, workshops, or small gatherings.

Ideal For

- Cultural Enthusiasts: With its prime location in Sarasota's arts district, the hotel is ideal to immerse yourself in the local culture, including theater, museums, and galleries.
- Business Travelers: The amenities and location make Hotel Indigo suitable for professionals seeking a stylish, convenient base with access to meeting spaces and downtown businesses.
- Leisure Travelers: Guests looking for a boutique experience with personalized service and distinctive style will find Hotel Indigo to be a perfect match.
- Pet Owners: The hotel's pet-friendly policy and amenities ensure that guests traveling with pets will have a comfortable and stress-free stay.

Hotel Indigo Sarasota offers a refreshing blend of local charm and modern convenience, wrapped in a stylish boutique package. Each aspect of the hotel, from its design and amenities to its location, is thoughtfully curated to enhance the experience of each guest, ensuring a memorable stay enriched by the vibrant cultural tapestry of Sarasota.

Carlisle Inn Sarasota

The Carlisle Inn Sarasota offers a distinct blend of Amish-inspired hospitality and modern comfort, positioned in a serene area of Sarasota that allows guests to enjoy both relaxation and the local attractions.

Location/Address

Located at 3727 Bahia Vista Street, Sarasota, Florida, Carlisle Inn Sarasota finds itself in a peaceful part of the city. The hotel's setting provides a unique contrast to the bustling downtown areas, offering a retreat-like atmosphere while still being close enough to enjoy the city's cultural and recreational activities.

Getting There

If you're arriving by air, the Sarasota-Bradenton International Airport is the closest major airport, approximately 20 minutes away by car. You can take the FL-780/Fruitville Road from the airport, follow it west, and then turn right onto Beneva Road, and left onto Bahia Vista Street to reach the hotel. If you're driving from Tampa, take I-75 South to exit 210 for FL-780/Fruitville Road, follow the same route westward to Beneva Road, and continue as above.

Key Amenities

- Spacious Accommodations: The Carlisle Inn offers spacious room options including suites with scenic views of the surrounding Amish and Mennonite community. The rooms are equipped with modern amenities while maintaining a decor that reflects the simplicity and craftsmanship synonymous with Amish traditions.
- Conference Facilities: Catering to business travelers or event planners, the Carlisle Inn provides ample meeting space equipped with modern audiovisual technology, making it ideal for conferences, retreats, and family reunions.
- Outdoor Pool and Fitness Center: A large outdoor swimming pool and a well-equipped fitness center are available to guests, offering ways to relax or stay active during their stay.
- Complimentary Breakfast: The hotel serves a complimentary breakfast featuring both local and traditional Amish favorites, a delightful way to start the day.

Ideal For

- Leisure Travelers: Those looking for a peaceful getaway will appreciate the quiet, comfortable setting of the Carlisle Inn, coupled with its proximity to Sarasota's attractions.
- Business Professionals: The extensive conference facilities and serene environment make it a perfect locale for business meetings and corporate retreats.
- Cultural Enthusiasts: Guests interested in the unique cultural heritage of the Amish and Mennonite communities will find the Carlisle Inn's setting and decor particularly engaging.

- Families: With spacious rooms and family-friendly amenities, the Carlisle Inn is well-suited for families traveling with children, offering comfort and convenience for all ages.

Carlisle Inn Sarasota merges traditional Amish values with contemporary amenities, creating a welcoming and tranquil atmosphere that stands out in Sarasota's accommodation offerings. This hotel not only promises comfort and relaxation but also provides a window into the rich cultural tapestry of the local Amish community, making it a unique and enriching experience for all who visit.

The Ringling Beach House

The Ringling Beach House offers a quaint and charming escape in the heart of Siesta Key, blending the comfort of a bed and breakfast with the independence of a boutique hotel. This inviting destination is ideal for a serene beachside retreat with easy access to Sarasota's vibrant cultural scene.

Location/Address

Located at 523 Beach Road, Sarasota, Florida, The Ringling Beach House is perfectly positioned just steps away from the world-famous Siesta Key Beach. Its prime location offers stunning seaside views and direct access to the soft, quartz sand beaches that have made Siesta Key a renowned destination.

Getting There

For guests flying into the area, the closest major airport is Sarasota-Bradenton International Airport, which is about a 25-minute drive from The Ringling Beach House. From the airport, you can head west on University Parkway, continue to Tamiami Trail, and follow signs to Stickney Point Road which leads directly to Siesta Key. Once on the island, a quick turn onto Beach Road will bring you to the property.

If you're driving from Tampa or St. Petersburg can reach Siesta Key in approximately an hour by taking I-75 South to exit 205 for Clark Road, and then following it west directly to the beaches of Siesta Key.

Key Amenities

- Private Access to Siesta Key Beach: You can enjoy private access to the sandy shores of Siesta Key Beach, just a few steps from their accommodations.
- Fully Equipped Accommodations: The Ringling Beach House features a variety of suites and cottages, each equipped with full kitchens, living areas, and private patios or balconies, allowing for a home-away-from-home experience.
- Outdoor Pool and Grill Area: Two heated outdoor pools and a grill area provide perfect spots for relaxation and family gatherings.
- Complimentary Bicycles: You can explore Siesta Key's charming village and beautiful landscapes with bicycles provided free of charge by the property.
- Beach Equipment: Complimentary beach chairs, umbrellas, and towels are available, ensuring a hassle-free beach day for all guests.

Ideal For

- Family Vacations: With its spacious suites and family-friendly amenities, The Ringling Beach House is perfectly suited for families looking to enjoy a beach vacation.
- Extended Stays: The fully equipped kitchens and comfortable living areas make this property ideal for guests planning longer stays in Siesta Key.
- Beach Enthusiasts: Anyone dreaming of a beachside holiday will find The Ringling Beach House's location and facilities ideal.
- Small Groups: The variety of accommodations and communal amenities like pools and grill areas make it a great choice for small groups or gatherings.

The Ringling Beach House encapsulates the essence of Siesta Key's laid-back beach lifestyle, offering guests a peaceful retreat with all the comforts of home.

Budget-Friendly Accommodations

The Ramada by Wyndham Sarasota Waterfront

The Ramada by Wyndham Sarasota Waterfront offers an affordable yet comfortable lodging option for visitors to Sarasota. Located on the waterfront, this hotel blends budget-friendly pricing with an array of amenities designed for both leisure and business travelers, ensuring a pleasant stay without breaking the bank.

Location/Address

The hotel is situated at 7150 N Tamiami Trail, Sarasota, Florida. This location places it directly on Sarasota Bay, offering scenic views and easy access to the water.

Getting There

For guests arriving by air, Sarasota-Bradenton International Airport is conveniently located just about 10 minutes from the hotel. To reach the hotel from the airport, take University Parkway west, then turn south on Tamiami Trail (US-41) and continue until you reach the hotel on your right.

If you are driving from Tampa, take I-75 South to exit 213 for University Parkway, then head west and follow the same route south on Tamiami Trail. The hotel's prominent location along this major roadway makes it easily accessible by car.

Key Amenities

- Waterfront Location: Enjoy stunning views of Sarasota Bay and easy access to waterfront activities.
- Outdoor Pool: The hotel features an outdoor pool that overlooks the bay, perfect for relaxation and family fun.
- On-Site Dining: You can dine at the on-site restaurant, which offers a variety of dishes and a view of the water.
- Fitness Center: A fully equipped fitness center is available for guests looking to stay active during their stay.
- Meeting and Event Facilities: The hotel offers several event spaces, ideal for business meetings, conferences, or social gatherings.

Ideal For

- Budget-Conscious Travelers: With its competitive pricing and valuable amenities, the Ramada by Wyndham Sarasota Waterfront is a great choice for travelers watching their budgets.
- Families: The outdoor pool and family-friendly dining options make it suitable for guests with children.

- Business Travelers: The proximity to the airport and available meeting spaces cater well to the needs of business guests.
- Visitors Seeking Waterfront Accommodations: You who enjoy being near the water will appreciate the hotel's location and the recreational opportunities it offers.

The Ramada by Wyndham Sarasota Waterfront proves that you do not need to sacrifice comfort for affordability. It provides all the necessary amenities for a fulfilling stay. This hotel ensures that you can enjoy the beauty and attractions of Sarasota without exceeding their travel budget.

Lantern Inn & Suites

The Lantern Inn & Suites offers a cozy and inviting atmosphere if you're seeking affordable accommodation without compromising on comfort and convenience. Located in Sarasota, this hotel is a popular choice for both short stays and extended visits due to its array of amenities and excellent location.

Location/Address

The Lantern Inn & Suites is located at 7251 N Tamiami Trail, Sarasota, Florida. This strategic positioning not only puts guests close to the Sarasota-Bradenton International Airport but also offers easy access to the beautiful Sarasota beaches and other key attractions.

Getting There

Reaching the Lantern Inn & Suites is straightforward for travelers. Those flying in will find the Sarasota-Bradenton International Airport conveniently close, just about 5 minutes north of the hotel. From the airport, guests can head south on Tamiami Trail (US-41) for a direct route to the hotel. If you're arriving by car from Tampa, the drive via I-75 South takes approximately an hour. Exit at University Parkway, proceed west and then take a right onto Tamiami Trail where the hotel will be located shortly after on the right-hand side.

Key Amenities

- Outdoor Pool: The hotel features a sparkling outdoor pool, perfect for a refreshing swim or lounging under the Florida sun.

- Complimentary Breakfast: You can start your day with a complimentary continental breakfast, featuring a variety of choices to suit different tastes and dietary needs.
- Pet-Friendly Accommodations: Traveling with pets is easier thanks to the hotel's pet-friendly policy, allowing guests to bring their furry friends along for their stay.
- Free High-Speed Internet: Stay connected with free high-speed internet access available throughout the property, ideal for both leisure and business travelers.
- Kitchenette in Select Rooms: Some rooms offer kitchenettes, providing convenience for guests who prefer to prepare their meals or those staying for longer periods.

Ideal For
- Budget-Conscious Travelers: The Lantern Inn & Suites is perfect if you're looking to maximize your travel budget without sacrificing essential amenities.
- Families: With spacious room options and a family-friendly pool, the hotel is well-suited for guests traveling with children.
- Extended Stay Visitors: The availability of kitchenette-equipped rooms makes this hotel a great choice for guests planning a longer visit to Sarasota.
- Pet Owners: Pet-friendly rooms ensure that no member of the family is left behind on trips to Sarasota.

With its comprehensive amenities and strategic location, the Lantern Inn & Suites ensures that guests enjoy a comfortable and convenient stay.

Siesta Key Palms Hotel

Siesta Key Palms Hotel offers a unique blend of comfort and serenity, making it an appealing choice if you're looking for an intimate and relaxed stay. Its tropical setting and modern amenities ensure a memorable experience in Sarasota, especially if you appreciate a close connection with nature.

Location/Address
The hotel is located at 1800 Stickney Point Rd, Sarasota, Florida. This prime location places it just minutes away from the famous Siesta Key

Beach, known for its stunning white sandy beaches and vibrant local community.

Getting There

Arriving at Siesta Key Palms Hotel is convenient, whether you are coming from nearby or traveling from a distance. The nearest major airport is Sarasota-Bradenton International Airport, located approximately 20 minutes away by car. From the airport, you can take University Parkway, turn south onto US-41, and then continue to Stickney Point Road, which leads directly to the hotel. If you're driving from Tampa, take I-75 South to exit 205 for Clark Road, head west to Stickney Point Road, and follow it until you reach the hotel.

Key Amenities

- Outdoor Pools: The hotel features two outdoor swimming pools, each surrounded by tropical gardens, providing a perfect place to relax and soak up the Florida sun.
- Private Patios: Many rooms include private patios or balconies that overlook the gardens, offering guests a personal oasis.
- Barbecue Grills: You have access to outdoor barbecue grills, ideal for an evening cookout under the stars.
- Laundry Facilities: On-site laundry facilities add convenience, particularly for longer stays.
- Parking: Complimentary parking is available, making it easy for guests to come and go as they please.

Ideal For

- Leisure Travelers: Those looking for a laid-back vacation will find Siesta Key Palms Hotel's tranquil environment perfect for a stay.
- Families: With spacious rooms and proximity to the beach and local attractions, the hotel is great for families enjoying a beach vacation.
- Eco-Conscious Travelers: The hotel's commitment to sustainability and its integration with the natural environment makes it particularly appealing to environmentally aware guests.
- Long-Term Visitors: Amenities like laundry facilities and kitchenettes in certain rooms make the hotel suitable for guests planning extended stays.

Thus, Siesta Key Palms Hotel provides a peaceful, comfortable, and environmentally conscious lodging option. Its blend of natural beauty, thoughtful amenities, and a prime location near Siesta Key Beach makes it an ideal choice for anyone looking to enjoy the natural and cultural offerings of the area.

Quality Inn Sarasota North

Quality Inn Sarasota North focuses on delivering reliable comfort and value to its guests. It simplifies the travel experience by providing essential hotel services and amenities, ensuring that every guest has a pleasant and hassle-free stay. The hotel's approach is centered around providing an efficient and friendly service in a location that allows easy access to Sarasota's main attractions.

Location/Address

Located at 4800 N Tamiami Trail, Sarasota, Florida, the hotel sits near the northern gates of Sarasota, positioned conveniently on one of the city's main thoroughfares. This strategic location offers both direct access to the Sarasota-Bradenton International Airport and easy routes to the vibrant downtown area and scenic waterfront.

Getting There

For air travelers, the Sarasota-Bradenton International Airport is less than a 5-minute drive away, making the hotel an ideal choice for proximity to the airport. Upon exiting the airport, take University Parkway west, turn right onto N Tamiami Trail, and the hotel will be shortly visible on the right-hand side.

Drivers from Tampa or St. Petersburg will find the hotel accessible via I-75 South, taking exit 213 for University Parkway, proceeding west, and then heading south on N Tamiami Trail. The hotel's location along this major road ensures it is easily identifiable.

Key Amenities

- Complimentary Breakfast: Start the day with a free continental breakfast that includes a variety of choices to cater to different tastes and dietary needs.
- Outdoor Pool: A well-maintained outdoor pool area allows guests to relax or enjoy a refreshing swim in a serene setting.

- Free High-Speed Internet: Stay connected with complimentary Wi-Fi available throughout the hotel.
- Business Center: Facilities include a business center equipped with computers and printers, suitable for both business travelers and those needing to handle personal affairs.
- Pet-Friendly Rooms: The hotel accommodates guests traveling with pets, offering specific rooms where pets are welcome.

Ideal For
- Budget-Conscious Travelers: With its competitive rates and essential amenities, the Quality Inn Sarasota North is perfect for travelers looking to maximize their budget without compromising on basic comforts.
- Business Travelers: The proximity to the airport and business amenities make it a convenient base for business activities or quick trips.
- Casual Vacationers: Leisure travelers will appreciate the easy access to Sarasota's attractions, including beaches, museums, and dining options.
- Pet Owners: Those traveling with pets will find the pet-friendly policy and the outdoor areas of the hotel suitable for a comfortable stay.

In essence, Quality Inn Sarasota North stands out as a practical choice for simplicity and efficiency. It offers a straightforward lodging experience that focuses on the essentials, making it a smart choice if you're visiting Sarasota for business or leisure.

Days Inn by Wyndham Sarasota Bay

Days Inn by Wyndham Sarasota Bay emphasizes straightforward, value-driven accommodations without compromising on quality and comfort. Known for its friendly service and welcoming atmosphere, the hotel aims to provide a pleasant stay experience for tourists and business travelers alike. It successfully combines a practical approach with attention to what matters most to guests – comfort, accessibility, and service.

Location/Address

Located at 5000 N Tamiami Trail, Sarasota, Florida, Days Inn by Wyndham Sarasota Bay is strategically positioned along one of the main arteries of the city. This location not only offers easy access to the attractions of downtown Sarasota but also places guests near the scenic areas along the Gulf Coast.

Getting There

If you're flying in, Sarasota-Bradenton International Airport is just a few minutes' drive away, making the hotel exceptionally convenient for air travelers. Simply head south on N Tamiami Trail (US-41) from the airport, and you will find the hotel on your left after a short drive.

If you're arriving by car from nearby cities such as Tampa or Naples, the hotel is accessible via I-75. Take exit 213 for University Parkway if coming from the north or south, proceed west, and then turn left onto N Tamiami Trail. The hotel will be on your right shortly after you pass the Sarasota Jungle Gardens.

Key Amenities

- Free Continental Breakfast: You can enjoy a complimentary breakfast each morning, featuring a variety of foods to start the day right.
- Outdoor Swimming Pool: A large, inviting pool area allows guests to relax or enjoy a swim in Florida's sunny weather.
- Free High-Speed Internet: Complimentary WiFi in all rooms and public areas ensures that you stay connected and entertained throughout your visit.
- Business Facilities: The hotel provides business travelers with access to business services including printing and faxing, along with meeting spaces for small groups.
- Pet-Friendly Accommodations: Traveling with pets is made easier with specific rooms designated for guests with furry companions.

Ideal For

- Economy Travelers: The hotel's focus on value and essential comforts makes it an ideal choice if you're traveling on a budget.

- Short Business Trips: Its proximity to the airport and essential business facilities suit those in town for quick business visits.
- Families: Family-friendly amenities, including the pool and the availability of spacious rooms, cater to those traveling with children.
- Pet Owners: The pet-friendly policy and easy access to outdoor areas make it a good option for guests who bring pets along on their travels.

Overall, Days Inn by Wyndham Sarasota Bay provides an economical yet comfortable accommodation choice, ensuring that guests have access to necessary amenities and a convenient base from which to explore or conduct business in Sarasota.

Chapter 6: Dining and Cuisine

Local Culinary Delights

For a taste of Sarasota, Florida, here are local culinary delights that showcase the rich flavors and diversity of the area's dining scene:

Stone Crab Claws - These are a must-try when in season (October to May). Often served chilled with a mustard sauce, stone crab claws are celebrated for their sweet, tender meat.

Grouper Sandwich - A Florida staple, the grouper sandwich features freshly caught grouper, typically grilled or fried, and served on a bun with lettuce, tomato, and tartar sauce.

Key Lime Pie - This classic Floridian dessert is made with a tangy lime custard, and a buttery graham cracker crust, and often topped with whipped cream or meringue.

Cuban Sandwich - Reflecting Tampa's influence, this sandwich is made with ham, roasted pork, Swiss cheese, pickles, mustard, and sometimes salami on Cuban bread.

Conch Fritters - Borrowed from Caribbean cuisine, these deep-fried delights are made with conch meat, bell peppers, onions, and celery, and served with a dipping sauce.

Sarasota Cioppino - A local take on the classic Italian-American seafood stew, incorporating the fresh catch from the Gulf, like snapper, shrimp, and clams, in a tomato and wine broth.

Alligator Bites - Often served as an appetizer, these are pieces of alligator meat that have been breaded and fried, served with dipping sauces like remoulade.

Smoked Mullet - A Gulf Coast tradition, this fish is typically smoked whole and enjoyed with a side of coleslaw or on crackers.

Spiny Lobster - Found in the warmer waters around Sarasota, spiny lobsters are featured in many local dishes, from grilled entrees to flavorful bisques.

Each of these dishes provides a unique flavor of Sarasota, perfect for culinary explorers looking to experience the local culture through its cuisine.

Top Restaurants and cafes

Fine Restaurants

Marina Jack

Marina Jack is renowned as a pinnacle of fine dining in Sarasota, Florida, offering a sophisticated ambiance combined with panoramic views of the Sarasota Bay. This upscale restaurant has become a landmark for both locals and visitors seeking an exceptional dining experience.

Origins of Marina Jack

The origins of Marina Jack trace back to its establishment as a key part of Sarasota's waterfront development. Over the years, it has evolved from a simple marina to a comprehensive dining and entertainment complex, embodying the spirit of Sarasota's maritime heritage and its commitment to luxury and quality.

Signature Dishes

- Marina Jack is celebrated for its exquisite menu, featuring a variety of dishes that cater to refined tastes. Signature dishes include:
- Blue Crab Bisque: A creamy and rich soup that delights with every spoonful, made with fresh local blue crab.
- Sesame Seared Tuna: Perfectly seared with a sesame crust, served with Asian-inspired accompaniments.
- Prime Rib: A classic dish, slow-roasted to achieve the perfect tenderness, and served with traditional sides.

Sourcing of Ingredients

The integrity of Marina Jack's menu is maintained through a rigorous ingredient sourcing policy. The restaurant prioritizes sustainable practices, sourcing seafood directly from local fishermen and procuring produce from nearby farms. This not only supports the local economy but also ensures the freshness and quality of the food served.

Location and Address

Marina Jack is located at 2 Marina Plaza, Sarasota, Florida

How to Get There

To visit Marina Jack

- From Sarasota-Bradenton International Airport: Drive south on US-41 for about 4 miles; the restaurant is on the right, at the heart of downtown Sarasota's bayfront.
- From I-75: Take exit 210 for Fruitville Road, drive west towards downtown, turn left on US-41 (Tamiami Trail), and continue to Marina Plaza.

Contact Information

- Phone: +1 (941) 365-4232
- Email: info@marinajacks.com

Unique Dining Experiences

Marina Jack offers more than just dining:

- Outdoor Patio: Enjoy meals al fresco on the patio overlooking the marina.
- Private Dining: Available for special occasions in a more intimate setting.
- Boat Docks: Arrive by boat and dock right at the restaurant for a truly unique approach.
- Live Entertainment: Regular live music enhances the dining experience, setting the mood with everything from jazz to soft rock.

Michael's On East

Michael's On East is a celebrated cornerstone of Sarasota's fine dining scene, revered for its sophisticated ambiance and impeccable service. Situated in the bustling heart of Sarasota, this restaurant offers a unique blend of gourmet American cuisine with a touch of international flair, served in a refined 1940s supper club atmosphere.

Origins of Michael's on East

Founded on April 27, 1987, by Michael Klauber and Philip Mancini, Michael's on East was established with a vision to create a top-tier dining destination that embodies the elegance and charm of classic Sarasota. Over the years, it has not only maintained its high standards but has also evolved into a culinary icon, celebrated for its innovative approach to fine dining and its commitment to excellence.

Signature Dish

The menu at Michael's on East is a testament to its culinary prowess, featuring an array of dishes that are both inventive and flavorful. A standout signature dish is the "*Colony Snapper*," which is delicately prepared with a unique blend of spices and accompanied by a side of the chef's specially crafted sauce. This dish not only highlights the restaurant's ability to innovate but also showcases its commitment to using fresh, local seafood.

Sourcing of Ingredients

At Michael's on East, there is a strong emphasis on sourcing ingredients locally and sustainably. The restaurant partners with regional fishermen and farmers to procure the freshest seafood and produce, ensuring that each dish is crafted with only the finest and most seasonal ingredients available. This practice not only enhances the flavor profile of their meals but also supports the local community and promotes environmental sustainability.

Location/Address

Michael's On East is conveniently located at 1212 South East Avenue, Sarasota, Florida.

How to Get There

To visit Michael's on East:

- From Sarasota-Bradenton International Airport: Drive south approximately 4 miles on US-41, turn right onto Bahia Vista Street, then left onto S. East Avenue.
- From Downtown Sarasota: Take Main Street to US-41 South, turn right on Bahia Vista Street, and left onto S. East Avenue.

Contact Information

For reservations or inquiries, Michael's on East can be contacted at:

Phone: +1 941-366-0007

Unique Dining Experiences

Michael's On East goes beyond conventional dining with several unique experiences:

- Wine Cellar Dinners: Enjoy a private dinner in the wine cellar surrounded by an impressive collection of wines.
- Live Music Nights: Experience the vibrant atmosphere with live music performances featuring local and visiting artists.
- Gourmet Cooking Classes: Participate in cooking classes led by expert chefs to learn the secrets behind some of Michael's on East's most famous dishes.

Indigenous

Indigenous stands out as a landmark in Sarasota's culinary landscape, celebrated for its dedication to sustainability and local sourcing. Nestled in the historic Towles Court artist colony, this restaurant merges innovative American cuisine with environmental consciousness, providing a unique dining experience that resonates deeply with eco-aware food enthusiasts.

Origins of Indigenous

Opened in 2011 by Chef Steve Phelps, Indigenous was born out of a passion for enhancing the dining scene in Sarasota with a focus on sustainability. Chef Phelps, a proponent of the slow food movement, envisioned a restaurant that not only serves food but also educates patrons about the importance of sustainability. Indigenous quickly gained acclaim, not just for its food but also for its commitment to the community and the environment.

Signature Dish

The signature dish at Indigenous is the "*Hogfish Snapper*," locally sourced and perfectly prepared to highlight its fresh, mild flavor. This dish is emblematic of Indigenous philosophy, showcasing local seafood caught in a manner that supports sustainable fishing practices.

Accompanied by seasonal sides that reflect the best of the region's produce, the Hogfish Snapper is a must-try for you.

Sourcing of Ingredients

Indigenous prides itself on a strict policy of sourcing locally and sustainably. The restaurant works closely with local fishermen, farmers, and artisans to procure ingredients that are not only fresh but also ethically produced. This farm-to-table approach ensures that the menu reflects the seasons and supports the local economy, while also minimizing the environmental impact of food production.

Location/Address

Indigenous is located at 239 S Links Ave, Sarasota, Florida

How to Get There

- From Downtown Sarasota, Indigenous is easily accessible. A short drive or a pleasant walk-through of Sarasota's picturesque streets will lead you to Towles Court. If you're arriving from outside the city:
- From Sarasota-Bradenton International Airport: Take US-41 southbound to Fruitville Road, head west, and then turn south onto Links Avenue.
- From I-75: Exit at Fruitville Road, head west towards downtown Sarasota and turn south onto Links Avenue.

Contact Information

To experience dining at Indigenous, reservations can be made through:

Phone: +1 (941) 706-4740

Unique Dining Experiences

Indigenous offers more than just dinner; it offers an immersive experience. With an open kitchen design, diners can watch as their meals are artfully prepared, fostering a deeper connection between the food and the guest. Regular culinary events, such as chef-led cooking classes and special tasting menus, further enrich the dining experience. The restaurant's involvement in community sustainability initiatives, such as local clean-up drives and educational programs, allows diners to participate in a larger movement towards environmental stewardship.

Casual Dining

Gecko's Grill & Pub

Gecko's Grill & Pub is a staple in the Sarasota casual dining scene, known for its friendly atmosphere and a menu that blends classic pub fare with local flavors. This restaurant caters to a diverse crowd, from families and sports enthusiasts to casual diners looking for quality food in a relaxed setting.

Origins of Gecko's Grill & Pub

Founded in 1992 by Mike Gowan and Mike Quillen, Gecko's Grill & Pub was conceived as a place where locals could gather for great food, sports, and community spirit. The founders, both Sarasota natives, wanted to create a venue that felt like an extension of a friend's home, welcoming and familiar. Their vision was realized and then some, as Gecko's has grown to multiple locations, becoming a beloved fixture in Sarasota.

Signature Dish

While Gecko's offers a variety of dishes, one standout is their award-winning burgers, each made with premium, never-frozen beef. A crowd favorite is the *"Gecko's Famous 'Smash' Burger"*, which features a perfectly cooked patty, secret sauce, and all the classic fixings on a toasted brioche bun. This burger exemplifies their commitment to quality and flavor and keeps patrons coming back for more.

Sourcing of Ingredients

Gecko's Grill & Pub emphasizes fresh, locally sourced ingredients. They partner with nearby farms and suppliers to stock their kitchens, ensuring that everything from the vegetables in their salads to the meats in their sandwiches is of the highest quality and freshness. This farm-to-table approach not only supports the local economy but also allows them to serve food that they can be proud of.

Location/Address

Gecko's Grill & Pub has several locations in Sarasota, but one of the most popular is located at 5585 Palmer Crossing Cir, Sarasota, Florida

How to Get There

To reach this location from downtown Sarasota:

- Drive south on US-41, turn right onto Clark Road, and continue until you reach the intersection with Honore Avenue. Gecko's is in the Palmer Crossing Shopping Center.
- Public Transport also runs regularly with a bus stop conveniently located near the shopping center.

Contact Information

Phone: +1 (941) 923-6061

Unique Dining Experiences

Gecko's Grill & Pub offers more than just dining:

- Sports Viewing: With numerous TVs and a lively sports bar atmosphere, it's the perfect place to watch a game.
- Family-Friendly: Gecko's offers a kid's menu and a welcoming environment that's great for family outings.
- Local Events: Regularly hosting events that support local charities and organizations, Gecko's is deeply embedded in the Sarasota community.
- Happy Hour Specials: Known for their daily Happy Hour, Gecko's offers great deals on drinks and appetizers, making it a popular after-work spot.

Siesta Key Oyster Bar

Siesta Key Oyster Bar, affectionately known as SKOB, is a vibrant cornerstone of Sarasota's dining scene, famed for its relaxed atmosphere and authentic seafood offerings. Located in the heart of Siesta Key Village, SKOB provides a perfect blend of casual dining with a special focus on fresh oysters and lively entertainment.

Origins of Siesta Key Oyster Bar

SKOB was established with a vision to create a friendly neighborhood spot where locals and tourists alike could enjoy fresh seafood and good times. It quickly became renowned for its engaging ambiance and quality dishes, embodying the laid-back lifestyle of Siesta Key.

Signature Dish

The menu at Siesta Key Oyster Bar features a variety of seafood, but the true highlight is their *Oysters Rockefeller*. These oysters are a gourmet treat, topped with a rich blend of spinach, bacon, and Pernod sauce, then broiled to perfection. This dish captures the essence of what SKOB stands for — fresh, flavorful, and fun.

Sourcing of Ingredients

Commitment to freshness is paramount at SKOB. The restaurant sources its oysters and other seafood directly from trusted local suppliers, ensuring that everything served is as fresh as possible. This dedication not only enhances the flavor of their dishes but also supports the sustainability of the local fishing industry.

Location/Address

Siesta Key Oyster Bar is conveniently located at 5238 Ocean Blvd, Sarasota, Florida

How to Get There

SKOB is easily accessible by various means:

- Driving: Located in Siesta Key Village, it is reachable via the Stickney Point Road bridge followed by a quick turn onto Midnight Pass Road and then Ocean Blvd.
- Public Transport: Multiple bus routes service the area, making stops within walking distance of the bar.
- Biking or Walking: If you're staying nearby, a scenic bike ride or a walk can be a great way to reach the restaurant.

Contact Information

To plan your visit or make inquiries, you can reach out through:

Phone: +1 (941) 346-5443

Unique Dining Experiences

SKOB isn't just about dining; it's about the experience. With its:

- Live Music: Almost every night, local bands and artists fill the space with music ranging from rock to reggae.

- Outdoor Seating: Enjoy your meal under the stars or a sunny blue sky on their expansive outdoor patio.
- Community Involvement: Regularly hosting events that support local causes, SKOB is deeply embedded in the community spirit of Sarasota.
- Themed Nights: From trivia nights to happy hour specials, there's always something happening at SKOB.

Drunken Poet Cafe

Drunken Poet Cafe is a celebrated destination in Sarasota, known for its eclectic blend of Thai cuisine and sushi. Located in the vibrant heart of downtown Sarasota, this restaurant provides a cozy yet sophisticated atmosphere where food and culture merge, offering diners a unique culinary experience.

Origins of Drunken Poet Cafe

Founded by Aporni Punyhotra, affectionately known as "Oy" to the locals, Drunken Poet Cafe opened its doors with the mission to introduce an innovative twist to traditional Thai and Japanese dishes. Since its inception, it has become a favorite among locals and tourists alike, who are drawn to its creative menu and warm ambiance.

Signature Dish

The Drunken Poet Cafe is renowned for its *Sexy Man Roll*, a sushi creation that perfectly encapsulates the restaurant's flair for combining traditional and modern tastes. It features fresh tuna, salmon, and avocado, topped with spicy mayo and eel sauce, creating a rich flavor profile that is both bold and delightful.

Sourcing of Ingredients

Sustainability and quality are pillars at Drunken Poet Cafe. The restaurant prides itself on using only the freshest ingredients, sourced from local markets and reputable suppliers who meet their high standards. This commitment ensures that each dish not only tastes good but is also made with responsibly sourced ingredients that support local producers.

Location/Address

The Drunken Poet Cafe is conveniently located at 1572 Main St, Sarasota, Florida

How to Get There

Arriving at Drunken Poet Cafe is straightforward:

- By Car: From I-75, take exit 210 for Fruitville Road and head west toward downtown Sarasota. Turn south on Lemon Avenue until you reach Main Street, then turn west. The cafe will be on your right.
- By Public Transport: Sarasota's bus network provides routes that stop near Main Street, making it easily accessible.

Contact Information

For more details or to make a reservation:

Phone: +1 941-955-8404

Unique Dining Experiences

Drunken Poet Cafe offers several distinctive dining experiences:

- Live Music Nights: Enjoy your meal accompanied by the soothing sounds of live music, featuring local artists that add to the vibrant atmosphere.
- Outdoor Seating: Experience al fresco dining on the patio, perfect for Sarasota's beautiful evenings.
- Culinary Workshops: Participate in sushi-making classes hosted by the restaurant, where guests can learn the art of sushi from experienced chefs.

Local Seafood

Owen's Fish Camp: A Taste of Old Florida

Owen's Fish Camp is an essential stop in Sarasota for anyone looking to experience the authentic flavor of Florida's Gulf Coast. Situated in the charming Burns Court district, this restaurant offers a laid-back atmosphere that perfectly captures the spirit of old Florida living. Here, guests can indulge in fresh, locally sourced seafood while enjoying the rustic and homey setting.

Origins of Owen's Fish Camp

The story of Owen's Fish Camp is deeply entwined with Sarasota's history. The restaurant is named after Owen Burns, a pivotal figure in Sarasota's development during the early 20th century. The banyan tree that stands proudly in front of the restaurant was reportedly a gift from Thomas Edison to Burns, adding to the historical significance of the location. This connection to local lore makes Owen's Fish Camp not just a place to eat but a place to experience Sarasota's rich past.

Signature Dish

Owen's Fish Camp is renowned for its Southern-inspired seafood dishes, with the *Low Country Boil* being a standout. This signature dish is a flavorful medley of shrimp, crab, potatoes, corn, and sausage, all boiled together with a blend of spices that evoke the essence of the South. It's a communal dish that encourages sharing and is best enjoyed with friends and family, making it a true reflection of the restaurant's homey ethos.

Sourcing of Ingredients

True to its roots, Owen's Fish Camp places a strong emphasis on sustainability and local sourcing. The seafood is delivered daily from local fishermen who use responsible fishing methods. This not only supports the local economy but also ensures that the seafood is as fresh as possible. The restaurant also sources its produce from local farms, emphasizing the quality and seasonality of the ingredients used in every dish.

Location/Address

Owen's Fish Camp is located at 516 Burns Court, Sarasota, Florida

How to Get There

Located in the historic Burns Court of Downtown Sarasota, Owen's Fish Camp is easily accessible:

- By Car: Drive down Main Street in downtown Sarasota, turn south onto Pineapple Avenue, then make a left onto Oak Street, which leads directly into Burns Court. Parking can be found along the street or in nearby public parking areas.
- By Public Transport: Several bus routes stop near Main Street, just a short walk from Burns Court.

Contact Information
Phone: +1 941-951-6936

Unique Dining Experiences
Owen's Fish Camp offers several unique dining experiences that make it a standout:

- Outdoor Banyan Tree: Dine under the sprawling branches of the historic banyan tree, a centerpiece of the restaurant's outdoor garden.
- Live Music: Enjoy live music performances in the evenings, featuring local musicians that enhance the casual and inviting atmosphere.
- Tire Swing: Adding to its old Florida charm, the tire swing hanging from the banyan tree offers a nostalgic touch that appeals to both kids and adults.
- Southern Hospitality: Experience genuine Southern hospitality with friendly service in a setting that feels like visiting a family home.

Dry Dock Waterfront Grill

Dry Dock Waterfront Grill, a renowned seafood restaurant, offers a pristine dining experience right on the shores of Sarasota Bay. Celebrated for its exceptional seafood and panoramic waterfront views, Dry Dock is a beloved destination for both locals and visitors seeking a taste of Florida's Gulf Coast.

Origins of Dry Dock Waterfront Grill
Founded in 1989, Dry Dock Waterfront Grill has established itself as a cornerstone of Sarasota's dining scene, embodying a commitment to quality and freshness. The restaurant's location at the south end of Longboat Key provides a scenic backdrop that complements its maritime theme, making it a picturesque spot for casual yet sophisticated dining.

Signature Dish
The Grouper Sandwich stands out as Dry Dock's signature dish, embodying the local culinary spirit with its fresh, locally sourced grouper. This beloved dish is served grilled, blackened, or fried, accompanied by a side of light, crispy fries and coleslaw, making it a must-try for any seafood aficionado visiting Sarasota.

Sourcing of Ingredients

Dry Dock Waterfront Grill prides itself on the freshness and quality of its ingredients. Seafood is sourced daily from local fisheries that practice sustainable fishing techniques, ensuring that each meal not only tastes good but also supports environmental stewardship. The restaurant also utilizes seasonal produce from nearby farms to complement its seafood offerings.

Location/Address

Dry Dock Waterfront Grill is located at 412 Gulf of Mexico Drive, Longboat Key, Florida

How to Get There

Located on Longboat Key, Dry Dock Waterfront Grill is easily accessible:

- By Car: From downtown Sarasota, take John Ringling Blvd (SR 789) north toward St. Armand's Circle, and continue following it as it turns into Gulf of Mexico Drive; the restaurant will be on your right.
- By Boat: Dock at Marker 6 in Sarasota Bay and enjoy direct access to the restaurant.

Contact Information

Phone: +1 (941) 383-0102

Unique Dining Experiences

Dry Dock offers a variety of unique dining experiences that enhance its allure:

- Waterfront Dining: Enjoy your meal on the deck overlooking Sarasota Bay, where dolphins and manatees are often sighted.
- Upstairs Dining Area: Offers elevated views of the bay, perfect for romantic dinners or special occasions.
- Live Cooking: Select evenings feature chefs preparing meals directly on the deck, offering diners a glimpse into the culinary artistry that goes into their dishes.
- Special Events and Catering: Dry Dock hosts a variety of events throughout the year, including wine tastings and holiday celebrations, and offers catering services for private events.

Walt's Fish Market

Walt's Fish Market is not just a restaurant but a landmark in Sarasota, Florida, celebrated for serving fresh seafood with a rich historical backdrop. This renowned establishment offers a genuine taste of Florida's seafood tradition, enhanced by a vibrant atmosphere that reflects over a century of culinary excellence.

Origins of Walt's Fish Market

Founded in 1918, Walt's Fish Market has deep roots in the Sarasota community. It began as a humble fish market and has evolved into a beloved seafood restaurant while still maintaining its market component. This dual function has allowed Walt's to remain a cornerstone of Sarasota's seafood scene, providing patrons with the freshest fish and a memorable dining experience.

Signature Dish

The Fresh Florida Stone Crab Claws are a signature dish at Walt's, available during the stone crab season from October to May. These claws are renowned for their sweetness and tender texture, served chilled with Walt's homemade mustard sauce. This dish not only highlights the local seafood but also showcases the restaurant's commitment to freshness and quality.

Sourcing of Ingredients

Walt's Fish Market takes pride in sourcing its seafood directly from local fishermen, many of whom have been working with the restaurant for generations. This close relationship ensures that only the freshest seafood, caught sustainably from the nearby Gulf waters, makes it to the table. The restaurant also supports local agriculture by incorporating seasonal produce from surrounding farms into its dishes.

Location/Address

Walt's Fish Market is located at 4144 S Tamiami Trl, Sarasota, Florida

How to Get There

Walt's Fish Market is easily accessible from various parts of Sarasota:

- By Car: Located on South Tamiami Trail, the restaurant is a short drive from downtown Sarasota. Head south on US-41, and you'll find Walt's on the right-hand side.
- By Public Transport: Several bus lines run along Tamiami Trail with stops near the restaurant, making it convenient when you opt for public transportation.

Contact Information

Phone: +1 (941) 921-4605

Unique Dining Experiences

Walt's Fish Market offers a variety of unique dining experiences that make it more than just a meal out:

- Outdoor Tiki Bar: Enjoy your seafood under the Florida sun or stars at the lively tiki bar, which often features live music and a great selection of local beers.
- Retail Market: Step into the retail side of Walt's to purchase fresh seafood to cook at home. The market also offers a selection of gourmet spices, sauces, and marinades.
- Cultural Events: Walt's frequently hosts events that celebrate local traditions and holidays, often featuring special menus and live entertainment.
- Cooking Demonstrations: Learn how to prepare seafood dishes with occasional cooking demonstrations led by the skilled chefs at Walt's, providing a hands-on culinary experience.

Cafe Amici

Cafe Amici is a celebrated Italian restaurant nestled in the heart of downtown Sarasota. Renowned for its authentic Italian dishes and warm, inviting atmosphere, Cafe Amici offers a slice of Italy in Florida, making it a favored destination for both locals and visitors who crave genuine Italian cuisine.

Origins of Cafe Amici

Cafe Amici was established in 1996 by Achille and Massimo Nigri, who aimed to bring the rich flavors and hearty spirit of Italian cooking to Sarasota. The restaurant quickly became a cultural staple, reflecting not only the culinary traditions of Italy but also the vibrant community of Sarasota.

Signature Dish

Among its extensive menu, Cafe Amici is particularly famous for its *Veal Marsala*. This dish, crafted with expertly sautéed veal and a rich Marsala wine sauce accompanied by a medley of forest mushrooms, encapsulates the essence of traditional Italian cooking. It stands as a testament to the restaurant's dedication to authenticity and quality.

Sourcing of Ingredients

At Cafe Amici, there is a strong emphasis on the authenticity and quality of ingredients. The kitchen uses imported Italian products alongside fresh, locally sourced produce, ensuring that each dish is both authentic and fresh. This blend of local and imported ingredients allows Cafe Amici to offer a genuine Italian dining experience while supporting local producers.

Location/Address

Cafe Amici is located at 1371 Main St, Sarasota, Florida

How to Get There

Cafe Amici is accessible and easy to locate in downtown Sarasota:

- By Car: Located on Main Street, it's easily reachable from any part of Sarasota. From I-75, take the Fruitville Road exit and head west towards downtown, then turn south on Orange Avenue and again west on Main Street.
- By Public Transport: Several bus routes serve the downtown area, making stops within walking distance of the restaurant.

Contact Information

Phone: +1 (941) 951-6896

Unique Dining Experiences

Cafe Amici offers several unique dining experiences that enhance its charm:

- Al Fresco Dining: Enjoy the beautiful Sarasota weather by dining outdoors on Cafe Amici's lovely patio.

- Wine Selections: With a vast selection of wines, primarily from Italy, you can enjoy perfect pairings with their meals.
- Italian-Themed Evenings: Regularly, the restaurant hosts Italian-themed nights that feature special menus and live music, providing a festive atmosphere that celebrates Italian culture.
- Cooking Classes and Wine Tastings: Engage in cooking classes led by experienced chefs or participate in wine-tasting events that showcase the best of Italian wines.

Selva Grill

Nestled in the vibrant heart of downtown Sarasota, Selva Grill stands out as a culinary gem, offering a sophisticated blend of Latin flavors with a modern twist. This restaurant is renowned for its dynamic atmosphere and a menu that creatively interprets traditional dishes from across Latin America.

Origins of Selva Grill

Selva Grill opened its doors in 2004 and quickly became a cornerstone of Sarasota's international dining scene. The concept was born from a desire to introduce a new style of Latin cuisine to the area, focusing on innovative presentations and complex flavors that go beyond the conventional.

Signature Dish

Selva Grill's menu is a celebration of Latin culinary art, with the *Ceviche de la Casa* standing out as a signature dish. This Peruvian-inspired ceviche features freshly caught local fish, marinated in lime juice with red onions, cilantro, and aji limo pepper, providing a perfect balance of tangy and spicy flavors that delight the palate.

Sourcing of Ingredients

At Selva Grill, there is a strong emphasis on the integrity and origin of ingredients. The restaurant sources its seafood from local and sustainable fisheries to ensure freshness and quality. Produce and other ingredients are often organic and sourced from local farms whenever possible, supporting the community and reducing the carbon footprint associated with food transport.

Location/Address
Selva Grill is conveniently located at 1345 Main St, Sarasota, Florida

How to Get There

Selva Grill is situated in downtown Sarasota, making it easily accessible by various means:

- By Car: From I-75, take exit 210 for Fruitville Road, head west towards downtown Sarasota, turn left onto Lemon Avenue, and then turn right onto Main Street.
- By Public Transport: The area is well-served by Sarasota's bus network, with several routes stopping near Main Street.

Contact Information
For inquiries or reservations at Selva Grill:

Phone: +1 (941) 362-4427

Unique Dining Experiences
Selva Grill offers more than just dining; it's a comprehensive sensory experience:

- Outdoor Seating: Enjoy the vibrant atmosphere of Main Street with comfortable and stylish outdoor seating options.
- Innovative Cocktails: The bar at Selva Grill is known for its creative cocktails that feature South American spirits and fresh, exotic ingredients.
- Special Events: The restaurant regularly hosts wine tastings, themed dinners, and cultural events that showcase the rich culinary traditions of Latin America.
- Artful Presentation: Each dish at Selva Grill is not only a feast for the palate but also for the eyes, with meticulous attention to presentation that elevates the dining experience.

Jpan Sushi & Grill

Nestled in the bustling heart of Sarasota, Jpan Sushi & Grill stands as a beacon of Japanese culinary excellence. Known for its refined approach to traditional Japanese dishes, Jpan offers an elegant dining experience that combines classic techniques with contemporary flavors, appealing to both connoisseurs and casual diners alike.

Origins of Jpan Sushi & Grill

Jpan Sushi & Grill was established with the intent to bring authentic Japanese cuisine to Sarasota, crafted under the guidance of skilled chefs. Since its opening, Jpan has dedicated itself to maintaining the integrity of traditional sushi making while infusing local character into its dishes, creating a unique dining environment that respects tradition yet embraces innovation.

Signature Dish

Among the exquisite offerings, Jpan's Volcano Roll stands out as a signature dish. This culinary masterpiece is carefully constructed with a base of sushi rice and fresh avocado, topped with a mix of spicy tuna and salmon, then drizzled with a special house-made spicy mayo and eel sauce. The dish is then lightly torched, giving it a smoky flavor that complements the freshness of the seafood.

Sourcing of Ingredients

Jpan Sushi & Grill prides itself on the quality and freshness of its ingredients. Seafood is sourced daily from trusted suppliers who adhere to sustainable fishing practices, ensuring that each piece of fish meets the highest standards of quality and freshness. Additionally, Jpan incorporates locally sourced vegetables and specialty items from Japan, balancing local and international flavors to perfection.

Location/Address

Jpan Sushi & Grill is located at 229 N Cattlemen Rd 61, Sarasota, Florida.

How to Get There

Jpan Sushi & Grill is located in the University Town Center area of Sarasota, making it conveniently accessible:

- By Car: From downtown Sarasota, take Fruitville Road east to Cattlemen Road, turn north, and continue until you reach the restaurant on your right.

- By Public Transport: Sarasota's bus network provides routes that stop near the University Town Center, a short walk from Jpan.

Contact Information

To experience Jpan Sushi & Grill or for more details:

Phone: +1 (941) 960-3997

Unique Dining Experiences

Jpan Sushi & Grill offers a range of unique dining experiences that elevate the traditional sushi dining model:

- Chef's Counter: Dine at the sushi bar and watch as chefs expertly prepare each dish, offering insights into the art of sushi making.
- Private Dining: Jpan offers a private dining area for special occasions, providing a more intimate experience.
- Seasonal Menus: The menu at Jpan changes with the seasons, reflecting the availability of the freshest ingredients and introducing diners to new flavors and techniques.
- Sake Pairings: Enhance your meal with a selection from Jpan's extensive sake collection, carefully chosen to complement the flavors of the dishes.

Vegetarian and Vegan Cuisine

Lila

Lila, located in the vibrant heart of downtown Sarasota, is a pioneer in the local dining scene, celebrated for its innovative approach to vegetarian and vegan cuisine. With a commitment to sustainability and health, Lila provides a refreshing dining experience that emphasizes organic and plant-centric dishes, appealing to a wide audience ranging from health-conscious eaters to those simply seeking a delicious meal.

Origins of Lila

Established with the vision of creating a space that serves creatively crafted vegetarian and vegan dishes, Lila opened its doors to the public, offering a menu that focuses on freshness and inventive culinary techniques. The restaurant quickly carved out a niche for itself by catering to a growing demand for healthy dining options in Sarasota while ensuring that each dish is as aesthetically pleasing as it is tasty.

Signature Dish

Among its diverse and flavorful menu, Lila's Hearts of Palm and Soybean Okara *'Crab Cake'* stands out as a signature dish. This innovative creation is a vegan take on the traditional crab cake, using hearts of palm and soybean okara to mimic the texture and flavor of crab, complemented by a wasabi tartar sauce that adds a delightful kick.

Sourcing of Ingredients

Lila is committed to sustainability and the ethical sourcing of ingredients. The restaurant sources organic produce from local farms, ensuring that the ingredients not only have minimal environmental impact but also support the local economy. Lila's dedication to organic and locally sourced ingredients is central to its mission, providing diners with fresh, nutrient-rich, and flavorful dishes.

Location/Address

Lila located at 1576 Main Street, Sarasota, Florida

How to Get There

Lila is easily accessible from anywhere in Sarasota:

- By Car: Located on Main Street in downtown Sarasota, it is easily reachable by car with several public parking options nearby.
- By Public Transport: Being in the downtown area, Lila is also accessible by various public transport routes, with bus stops conveniently located close to the restaurant.

Contact Information

Phone: +1 941-296-1042

Unique Dining Experiences

Lila offers several unique aspects that enhance the dining experience:

- Open Kitchen Design: The restaurant features an open kitchen, allowing diners to watch as their meals are thoughtfully prepared.

- Seasonal Menus: Reflecting the changing seasons, Lila regularly updates its menu to take advantage of the freshest available produce and introduce new, innovative dishes.
- Wine Pairings: Lila offers an extensive selection of organic and biodynamic wines from around the world, carefully selected to complement their dishes.
- Eco-Friendly Practices: Beyond the kitchen, Lila is dedicated to sustainability throughout its operations, utilizing eco-friendly materials and practices in every facet of its business.

Veg

Veg stands as a beacon for vegan and vegetarian cuisine in Sarasota, offering a delightful array of dishes that cater to a health-conscious audience. Located in the vibrant Gulf Gate area, this restaurant has carved out a niche for itself by providing innovative plant-based meals that tantalize the taste buds without compromising on flavor or creativity.

Origins of Veg

Founded with a mission to provide delicious and nutritious food that supports a vegan lifestyle, Veg has quickly become a hub for both vegans and non-vegans alike. The restaurant opened its doors with the aim of bringing a fresh perspective to plant-based dining, focusing on wholesome, inventive, and satisfying dishes.

Signature Dish

Veg's menu is a testament to its innovative approach, but one dish, in particular, has gained a following: the Jackfruit Tacos. These tacos are made with seasoned jackfruit, which mimics the texture of pulled pork, topped with a vibrant slaw and avocado cream, offering a flavorful and satisfying experience that's both vegan and gluten-free.

Sourcing of Ingredients

Veg is committed to sustainability and ethical food practices. The restaurant sources its ingredients from local organic farms and suppliers who align with its environmental and health values. This approach ensures that the dishes are not only fresh but also support local agriculture and reduce the carbon footprint associated with food transport.

Location/Address

Veg is located at 2164 Gulf Gate Drive, Sarasota, Florida

How to Get There

Veg is situated in the Gulf Gate Estates, making it easily accessible:

- By Car: From central Sarasota, take Clark Road heading south, turn right on Gateway Avenue, and then another right onto Gulf Gate Drive.
- By Public Transport: Sarasota's bus network provides routes that stop near Gulf Gate Drive, making Veg accessible by public transportation.

Contact Information

Phone: +1 (941) 312-6424

Unique Dining Experiences

Veg offers a range of unique dining experiences that set it apart:

- Outdoor Seating: Enjoy the beautiful Sarasota weather in Veg's charming outdoor seating area.
- Monthly Specials: Each month, Veg introduces new dishes based on seasonal ingredients, giving diners new flavors to explore.
- Community Events: Veg regularly participates in local food festivals and vegan meetups, helping to foster a community around plant-based eating.
- Health and Wellness Workshops: The restaurant hosts events focused on health and wellness, including cooking demonstrations and nutrition talks, aligning with its mission to promote a healthy lifestyle.

Ionie's Raw Food Cafe

Ionie's Raw Food Cafe, situated in the heart of Sarasota, Florida, is a haven for a nutritious dining experience that is both delightful and rejuvenating. This establishment is renowned for its commitment to providing meals that are not only vegan and raw but also infused with flavors that appeal to all palates.

Origins of Ionie's Raw Food Cafe

Ionie's Raw Food Cafe was established with the philosophy of healing and nourishing the body through food. It opened its doors with the mission to offer a menu that supports wellness and a healthy lifestyle, making it a pioneer in the raw food movement in Sarasota. The cafe quickly became a favorite among health-conscious diners, thanks to its innovative approach to raw vegan cuisine.

Signature Dish

The cafe is celebrated for its *Raw Lasagna*, a creative and flavorful dish that epitomizes the essence of raw food cuisine. This dish layers thinly sliced zucchini with a rich walnut meat substitute, topped with a sundried tomato marinara and a creamy cashew nut cheese, offering a complex texture and depth of flavor that surprises and delights diners.

Sourcing of Ingredients

At Ionie's Raw Food Cafe, the emphasis is on organic, locally sourced, and seasonal ingredients. The cafe partners with local farmers and suppliers to ensure that the produce used is of the highest quality and freshness. This commitment not only enhances the nutritional value of the dishes but also supports the local community and promotes sustainable practices.

Location/Address

Ionie's Raw Food Café is located at 1241 Fruitville Rd, Sarasota, Florida

How to Get There

Ionie's Raw Food Cafe is conveniently located in downtown Sarasota, making it easily accessible:

- By Car: From I-75, take exit 210 for Fruitville Road and proceed west towards downtown Sarasota. The cafe is located just before reaching Tamiami Trail.
- By Public Transport: Sarasota's bus network services the downtown area, with stops near Fruitville Road close to the cafe.

Contact Information

To learn more about Ionie's Raw Food Cafe or to make a reservation:

Phone: +1 (941) 320-0504

Unique Dining Experiences

Ionie's Raw Food Cafe offers several distinctive dining experiences:

- Garden Patio Dining: Enjoy your meal in a serene garden setting, surrounded by lush greenery and soothing water features, which enhance the peaceful ambiance.
- Health and Wellness Workshops: The cafe regularly hosts workshops and seminars focusing on health, nutrition, and wellness, providing diners not just a meal, but an opportunity to learn and grow in their health journeys.
- Live Food Demonstrations: Experience the preparation of raw foods firsthand during live demonstrations that educate diners on the benefits and techniques of raw food preparation.
- Detox and Cleanse Programs: Ionie's offers guided detox programs, which include meal plans featuring items from their menu, aiding patrons in their health and wellness goals.

Munchies 420 Cafe

Located in the vibrant Gulf Gate area of Sarasota, Munchies 420 Cafe offers a unique dining experience characterized by its eclectic menu and laid-back atmosphere. Known for its late-night service and hearty comfort food, this cafe has become a favorite among locals and visitors looking for a casual place to satisfy their cravings at almost any hour.

Origins of Munchies 420 Cafe

Munchies 420 Cafe was established in 2004 with a straightforward mission: to provide delicious, satisfying food paired with a fun and friendly environment. Its name, a playful nod to the cannabis culture, hints at the informal and quirky nature of the cafe, which has always aimed to be a place where patrons can relax and enjoy good food and good times.

Signature Dish

The Fat Sandy sandwich has gained notoriety as Munchies 420 Cafe's signature dish. This monstrous creation features chicken fingers, mozzarella sticks, onion rings, and French fries, all stuffed into a sandwich, making it the epitome of comfort food. It's particularly popular among those with a hearty appetite and a taste for indulgence.

Sourcing of Ingredients

Munchies 420 Cafe takes pride in sourcing high-quality ingredients to elevate its array of comfort foods. While the focus is on creating satisfying and flavorful dishes, the cafe ensures that all ingredients meet their standards for freshness and quality, whether they're locally sourced or selected from top suppliers.

Location/Address

Munchies 420 Café is located at 6639 Superior Ave, Sarasota, Florida

How to Get There

Located just off the Tamiami Trail in the Gulf Gate area, Munchies 420 Cafe is easily accessible:

- By Car: From downtown Sarasota, take the Tamiami Trail (US-41) south to Stickney Point Road, turn left, and then take another left onto Superior Avenue. The cafe is a short drive down on the right.
- By Public Transport: Sarasota County Area Transit (SCAT) buses serve the area with stops along Superior Avenue, making it convenient if you're using public transportation.

Contact Information

- Phone: +1 (941) 929-9893
- Email: munchies420cafe.site@gmail.com

Unique Dining Experiences

Munchies 420 Cafe stands out not just for its food but also for the unique experiences it offers:

- Late-Night Dining: One of the few places in Sarasota open until 4:20 am, catering to night owls and those with late-night munchies.
- Eclectic Decor: The interior is filled with colorful artwork and quirky decorations that reflect the cafe's fun and casual ethos.
- Live Music and Events: Regular events including live music and trivia nights contribute to a lively and engaging atmosphere.
- Outdoor Seating: Enjoy Sarasota's balmy evenings in the cafe's outdoor seating area, perfect for a relaxed meal under the stars.

Gentile Bros. Authentic Cheesesteaks

Gentile Bros. Authentic Cheesesteaks brings a taste of Philadelphia to Sarasota, Florida, offering an authentic cheesesteak experience that rivals those found in the City of Brotherly Love. Known for its dedication to authenticity and quality, Gentile Bros. has become a beloved spot for both locals and visitors craving genuine Philly cheesesteaks.

Origins of Gentile Bros. Authentic Cheesesteaks

Established in 2012 by the Gentile family who moved from South Philadelphia to Sarasota, the restaurant was founded with a commitment to bring true Philadelphia cheesesteaks to the Gulf Coast. Utilizing traditional recipes and ingredients sourced directly from Philadelphia, Gentile Bros. quickly established itself as the go-to place for authentic cheesesteaks in Sarasota.

Signature Dish

The Classic Philly Cheesesteak is the signature dish at Gentile Bros. This sandwich features thinly sliced ribeye steak, expertly cooked and layered with melted cheese (choice of American, Provolone, or Cheez Whiz) on a soft Amoroso roll, also shipped from Philadelphia. Patrons can customize their cheesesteak with onions, peppers, mushrooms, and other toppings to suit their tastes.

Sourcing of Ingredients

Gentile Bros. prides itself on the authenticity and quality of its ingredients. The ribeye steak is carefully selected for its flavor and tenderness, ensuring the perfect texture for each sandwich. Rolls are sourced from Amoroso's, a famed Philadelphia bakery, to guarantee that every bite is as genuine as those found in Philly cheesesteak joints. Additional ingredients, such as cheese and toppings, are sourced locally when possible, balancing authenticity with fresh, high-quality produce.

Location/Address

Gentile Bros. Authentic Cheesesteaks is located at 7523 S Tamiami Trail, Sarasota, Florida

How to Get There

Gentile Bros. is conveniently located on the South Tamiami Trail, making it easily accessible:

- By Car: From downtown Sarasota, head south on US-41/Tamiami Trail. The restaurant is located in the South Trail Plaza just past the intersection with Stickney Point Road.
- By Public Transport: Sarasota County Area Transit (SCAT) provides bus services that run along the Tamiami Trail with stops near the restaurant.

Contact Information

Phone: (941) 926-0441

Unique Dining Experiences

Gentile Bros. offers more than just great food; it provides a unique dining experience that includes:

- Philadelphia Sports Memorabilia: The walls of the restaurant are adorned with memorabilia from Philadelphia sports teams, creating a nostalgic atmosphere for Philly natives and sports fans.
- Outdoor Seating: Enjoy your cheesesteak outdoors in the pleasant Sarasota weather, adding a Floridian twist to this Philly classic.
- Family-Owned Hospitality: Experience the warm, friendly service that only a family-owned business can offer, making every visit feel like stepping into a home away from home.

El Toro Bravo

Nestled in the heart of Sarasota, El Toro Bravo stands out as a bastion of authentic Southwest Mexican cuisine. Since its opening in 2005, this family-owned restaurant has become a local favorite, renowned for its welcoming atmosphere and commitment to serving traditional Mexican dishes crafted with genuine flavors and ingredients.

Origins of El Toro Bravo

El Toro Bravo was founded by a Sarasota local who envisioned bringing the rich, vibrant tastes of Southwest Mexico to Florida. The founder's passion for Mexican cuisine, coupled with a dedication to authenticity, has propelled El Toro Bravo into a well-loved dining destination that locals and tourists flock to for a taste of genuine Mexican dishes.

Signature Dish

At the heart of El Toro Bravo's menu is the Chimichanga, a deep-fried burrito that epitomizes the fusion of flavor and texture that Mexican cuisine is known for. Filled with a choice of chicken, beef, or pork, and combined with refried beans and cheese, then topped with lettuce, guacamole, sour cream, and a rich tomato salsa, this dish is a perennial favorite among patrons.

Sourcing of Ingredients

El Toro Bravo prides itself on the authenticity and quality of its ingredients. Many of the key ingredients are imported directly from Mexico to ensure the dishes maintain their traditional flavor profiles. Additionally, the restaurant supports local agriculture by sourcing fresh produce from nearby farms whenever possible, thereby guaranteeing the freshness of their dishes while supporting the local economy.

Location/Address

El Toro Bravo is located at 3218 Clark Rd, Sarasota, Florida

How to Get There

El Toro Bravo is located on Clark Road, a major thoroughfare in Sarasota, making it easily accessible:

- By Car: From downtown Sarasota, head south on Tamiami Trail, turn right onto Stickney Point Road and then left onto Clark Road. The restaurant will be on your left.
- By Public Transport: Sarasota County Area Transit (SCAT) provides bus services with routes that pass near Clark Road, making the restaurant accessible.

Contact Information

Phone: +1 941-924-0006

Unique Dining Experiences

El Toro Bravo offers several unique experiences that enhance its appeal:

- Outdoor Patio Dining: Enjoy Sarasota's beautiful weather by dining on the spacious outdoor patio, which offers a relaxed and casual atmosphere.
- Live Music Nights: Regular live music events feature local bands that play traditional Mexican and Latin American music, adding to the authentic dining experience.
- Tequila Tastings: The restaurant hosts tequila-tasting events that allow guests to explore the rich variety of tequilas sourced directly from Mexico.
- Family-friendly Atmosphere: El Toro Bravo provides a welcoming environment that is perfect for family gatherings, with a menu that caters to all ages.

Cooking Classes in Sarasota

Sarasota's thriving culinary scene is not just about dining but also about learning and experiencing the joy of cooking with farm-fresh ingredients. Several establishments in Sarasota offer cooking classes that focus on farm-to-table concepts, providing locals and visitors with the opportunity to engage directly with the food they eat, from sourcing to preparation.

Origins of Farm-to-Table Cooking Classes

The farm-to-table movement in Sarasota gained momentum as part of a broader national trend towards sustainability and healthier eating. Cooking classes started as a way to educate the community about the benefits of using local ingredients and to foster a deeper connection between farmers and consumers. These classes have grown in popularity as they provide hands-on experience with high-quality, local produce and teach participants how to create delicious, nutritious meals.

Signature Dishes and Ingredients

Each cooking class focuses on different dishes, often depending on the season and the availability of local ingredients. Common themes include:

- Seasonal Vegetarian Delights: Dishes that highlight the versatility of vegetables, such as farm-fresh salads or vegetable-centric entrees.
- Local Seafood Preparations: Cooking with freshly caught fish, demonstrating techniques like grilling, searing, or making ceviche.

- Artisanal Pasta Making: Using local eggs and herbs to make homemade pasta from scratch.

The ingredients used in these classes are sourced from local farms, markets, and sometimes directly from the cooking school's garden, ensuring that participants work with the freshest and most nutritious ingredients.

Locations and Accessibility

➤ The Rosemary: Offers cooking classes that teach traditional American and international dishes using local ingredients.
- Location: 511 N Orange Ave, Sarasota, Florida
- Getting There: Located in downtown Sarasota, accessible by car and public transport with ample parking in the area.
➤ Tableseide Cooking Classes: Known for a more diverse array of classes including Mediterranean cooking and plant-based menus.
- Location: Various locations depending on the class, often held in larger kitchens or farms around Sarasota.
- Getting There: Details are provided upon registration, with each location chosen for its accessibility and facilities.

Contact Information

- The Rosemary: +1 941-955-7600
- Tableseide Group: +1 941-552-9650

Unique Dining Experiences

These cooking classes offer more than just culinary education; they provide a holistic dining experience:

- Farm Tours: Some classes include a tour of a local farm, where participants can pick their ingredients.
- Wine Pairings: Classes often include sessions on how to pair dishes with local or international wines.
- Chef Demonstrations: Experienced chefs demonstrate techniques and share secrets on how to bring out the best in local ingredients.
- Community Table: After cooking, participants often sit down together to enjoy the meal they've prepared, fostering a sense of community and shared accomplishment.

Chapter 7: Cultural Heritage

Festivals and Cultural Events

Sarasota Film Festival

Origins

The Sarasota Film Festival (SFF) was founded in 1998 with the aim of supporting and promoting independent filmmakers while enriching Sarasota's cultural landscape. Over the years, it has grown into a major event on the independent film circuit, attracting filmmakers, critics, and movie lovers from around the world. The festival is a celebration of cinematic artistry, showcasing a diverse range of films, from feature-length movies to shorts and documentaries.

Date of Event

The Sarasota Film Festival typically takes place annually in April. Specific dates vary each year, and information can be found on the festival's official website or by contacting the festival's organizing committee directly.

Significance

The significance of the Sarasota Film Festival extends beyond entertainment. It serves as a platform for cultural dialogue and community engagement, fostering an appreciation for the arts within Sarasota and beyond. The festival also provides independent filmmakers with a valuable venue for showcasing their work, offering them exposure and the opportunity to network with industry professionals. Moreover, SFF contributes to the local economy by attracting tourists and promoting Sarasota as a destination for cultural tourism.

Unique Attractions

One of the unique aspects of the Sarasota Film Festival is its commitment to social issues and educational outreach. The festival often features films that address critical topics such as social justice, the environment, and human rights, sparking discussions and encouraging action.

Additionally, SFF holds a variety of special events, including a Filmmaker's Tribute, a Cinema Tropicale celebration, and panel discussions with filmmakers, actors, and industry experts.

Typical Activities and Performances

During the festival, attendees can enjoy a wide range of activities:

- Screenings: A diverse array of films are shown at various venues throughout Sarasota, including world premieres, undiscovered gems, and critically acclaimed works.
- Q&A Sessions: Many screenings are followed by Q&A sessions where filmmakers and actors discuss their work and answer questions from the audience, providing deeper insights into the creative process.
- Workshops and Masterclasses: SFF offers workshops and masterclasses led by seasoned filmmakers and industry professionals, covering topics from directing to scriptwriting to cinematography.

Notable Traditions

A notable tradition of the Sarasota Film Festival is the "*In Conversation With*" series, which features intimate discussions with prominent actors and filmmakers. These events provide a rare opportunity for festival-goers to hear from leading figures in the film industry in a more personal, relaxed setting. Past guests have included renowned personalities such as Sophia Loren, Kevin Bacon, and Stanley Tucci, making each session a highlight of the festival.

The Sarasota Film Festival not only celebrates the art of filmmaking but also enriches Sarasota's cultural fabric. Through its diverse screenings, educational initiatives, and community engagement, SFF continues to be an integral part of Sarasota's cultural heritage, drawing attention to the power of film as a medium for storytelling and social change.

Sarasota Music Festival

Origins

The Sarasota Music Festival (SMF) is a renowned classical music festival that began in 1965. Founded by the Sarasota Concert

Association, the festival was initially a small-scale event aimed at enriching the local cultural scene. Over the decades, it has evolved into one of the most prestigious classical music festivals in the United States, known for its educational focus and high-caliber performances.

Date of Event

The Sarasota Music Festival typically takes place over three weeks in June. It features a packed schedule of performances, masterclasses, and rehearsals that transform Sarasota into a hub for classical music enthusiasts. Exact dates for the festival can be found on the Sarasota Orchestra's website, which hosts and organizes the event each year.

Significance

The festival is significant not only for its contributions to cultural enrichment in Sarasota but also for its educational mission. It attracts young musicians from around the world to learn from distinguished artists. The SMF is celebrated for fostering the next generation of classical musicians, providing them with invaluable mentorship and performance opportunities. Additionally, the festival significantly boosts local tourism and economy, drawing classical music fans to Sarasota each summer.

Unique Attractions

One of the unique features of the Sarasota Music Festival is its blend of student and professional performances. The festival participants, who are advanced students and pre-professional musicians, play alongside seasoned professionals in orchestral, chamber, and solo settings. This mentorship and collaboration culminate in public performances, offering a rare and enriching experience for both performers and audiences.

Typical Activities and Performances

- Student Recitals: These showcase the talents of the festival's participants, featuring solo and small ensemble pieces.
- Faculty Concerts: Performed by visiting artists and teachers, these concerts are a highlight of the festival, offering performances at an extraordinarily high level.

- Masterclasses and Lectures: Public masterclasses provide insight into the artistic process as faculty members coach students on technique, expression, and performance practice.

Notable Traditions

A notable tradition of the Sarasota Music Festival is the "Festival Fridays" series, where students and faculty come together to perform challenging and diverse repertoire in orchestral concerts. These events are particularly special as they display the cumulative work of the festival's rigorous training and rehearsals. Another cherished tradition is the final grand concert, which serves as both a showcase of the festival's achievements and a celebration of classical music.

Sarasota Powerboat Grand Prix Festival

Origins

The Sarasota Powerboat Grand Prix Festival first made waves in 1985, initially established as a fundraising event to support local charitable organizations. It quickly evolved into one of the most anticipated annual events in Sarasota, bringing together the thrill of powerboat racing with community spirit and philanthropy. The festival's mission extends beyond entertainment, focusing on raising funds for Suncoast Charities for Children, making it a pivotal event with a purpose.

Date of Event

The Sarasota Powerboat Grand Prix Festival typically takes place over a week around late June to early July. The exact dates vary each year, but the festival always culminates with the grand powerboat races on the final weekend. Detailed schedules and event dates are published annually on the festival's official website and local tourism boards.

Significance

This festival is significant not just for its high-speed races but also for its impact on the local community. It has become a major fundraiser, contributing millions of dollars to support children, teens, and adults with special needs through the Suncoast Charities for Children. Moreover, it significantly boosts the local economy by attracting thousands of tourists to Sarasota, filling hotels, restaurants, and beaches.

Unique Attractions

- Powerboat Races: The highlight of the festival, these races feature some of the world's fastest and most powerful boats competing along the Lido Beach coastline. Spectators can watch these thrilling races from the shore or aboard boats anchored near the racecourse.
- Festival Parade of Boats: Before race day, a parade of all participating boats through downtown Sarasota provides a close-up view of the impressive machines and their teams.
- Boat and Personal Watercraft Fun Run: Open to all boaters, this event allows participants to navigate local waters in a non-competitive environment, enjoying the beauty of Sarasota's waterways.

Typical Activities and Performances

- Kickoff Party: The festival begins with a party that includes live music, food, and introductions of the race teams to the community.
- VIP Race Viewing Parties: For a premium experience, spectators can enjoy the races from exclusive parties held on rooftops and waterfront venues offering food, drinks, and unobstructed views of the action.
- Fireworks Display: A spectacular fireworks show over Sarasota Bay marks the conclusion of the festival, lighting up the sky in celebration of the event's success.

Notable Traditions

A cherished tradition of the Sarasota Powerboat Grand Prix Festival is the "*Miss Powerboat Grand Prix*" contest, where contestants compete for the title based on community involvement and charity support rather than just appearance. Another long-standing tradition is the community day, where local residents and visitors can meet the racers, see the boats up close, and participate in interactive activities and educational workshops related to marine sports and safety.

Location/Address

Centennial Park and Lido Beach serve as the primary venues for the festival events and races.

Centennial Park Address: 1059 N Tamiami Trail, Sarasota, Florida

How to Get There

Centennial Park is accessible via Tamiami Trail, one of Sarasota's main thoroughfares. Lido Beach offers ample space for spectators if you're attending the boat races. Public transport and parking options are available, with additional shuttles often running on race days to accommodate the large crowds.

The Sarasota Powerboat Grand Prix Festival is a hallmark event that combines high-energy sports with community engagement and philanthropy. Its lasting appeal not only draws competitive racers from around the globe but also unites the Sarasota community in support of a noble cause, making it a significant cultural and charitable fixture in the region.

Sarasota Chalk Festival

Origins

The Sarasota Chalk Festival is a vibrant celebration of street art that began in 2007. Founded by Denise Kowal, the festival started as a local initiative to bring public art to the streets of Sarasota and quickly grew into an internationally recognized event. It was the first international street painting festival in the USA, attracting artists and spectators from around the world to engage in this unique form of artistic expression.

Date of Event

The Sarasota Chalk Festival typically takes place annually in November, when the weather is ideal for outdoor activities. The dates can vary slightly each year, so attendees are encouraged to check the festival's official website for the most current information.

Significance

The festival not only beautifies the city with intricate and ephemeral works of art but also serves as a significant cultural event that promotes creativity and community engagement. It highlights the importance of public art and its ability to transform spaces and inspire community interaction. Additionally, the event supports artists by providing them with a platform to showcase their skills and gain international exposure.

Unique Attractions

- Pavement Art: Artists use chalk to create detailed and elaborate temporary artworks directly on the pavement, transforming ordinary streets into open-air museums.
- 3D Chalk Art: One of the festival's highlights is the stunning 3D chalk art, where artists create mind-bending optical illusions that appear to rise from or sink into the ground.
- Themed Creations: Each year, the festival has a theme that inspires the artworks, adding a cohesive narrative to the entire event that enhances the viewer's experience.

Typical Activities and Performances

- Artist Demonstrations: Spectators can watch as artists from various backgrounds and skill levels work on their creations from start to finish.
- Art Workshops: The festival offers chalk art workshops for both beginners and experienced artists, taught by professional street painters.
- Music and Entertainment: Live music and performances add to the festive atmosphere, with local bands and performers adding a soundtrack to the visual spectacle.
- Children's Activities: Special sections and activities are dedicated to young artists, making it a family-friendly event where children can try their hand at chalk art.

Notable Traditions

One of the most beloved traditions of the Sarasota Chalk Festival is the *"Going Vertical"* initiative, where artists create permanent murals on buildings around the city. This initiative not only extends the impact of the festival beyond its temporary nature but also leaves a lasting artistic legacy in Sarasota.

Location/Address

Historic Burns Square is located at Downtown Sarasota, Florida

How to Get There

Burns Square is located in downtown Sarasota, making it easily accessible by car or public transportation. Parking is available in nearby lots and streets, and several bus routes stop within walking distance of the festival site.

The Sarasota Chalk Festival is more than an art event; it is a celebration of artistic talent, community, and the transient beauty of street painting. Each year, it draws crowds, artists, and media attention, spotlighting Sarasota as a cultural hub and fostering a greater appreciation for the transformative power of public art.

Chapter 8: Shopping and Souvenirs

Best Shopping Districts

When visiting Sarasota, exploring its vibrant shopping districts is a must-do activity. These districts offer a diverse range of shopping experiences, ensuring you'll find something to suit your style and preferences.

St. Armands Circle

Situated just across the Ringling Bridge from downtown Sarasota, St. Armands Circle is a charming and walkable shopping district with a European flair. As you approach this circular enclave, you'll be captivated by its elegant architecture and lush landscaping. Getting to St. Armands Circle is a breeze. Simply head west on John Ringling Boulevard from downtown Sarasota, and you'll find yourself at the entrance to this shopper's paradise.

St. Armands Circle boasts a collection of boutique shops, art galleries, and upscale restaurants. Whatever you're looking for, you're sure to find it here. From trendy fashion boutiques to specialty stores offering unique gifts and home decor, the options are plentiful. As you stroll along the palm-lined sidewalks, you'll have the opportunity to discover one-of-a-kind items that will serve as lasting mementos of your Sarasota vacation.

Beyond its diverse shopping offerings, St. Armands Circle is renowned for its culinary delights. Once you've worked up an appetite, numerous restaurants with outdoor seating beckon you to indulge in a leisurely meal. From casual eateries serving fresh seafood to fine dining establishments with international cuisine, the dining options are as varied as the shopping experiences. Be sure to save room for a sweet treat from one of the delightful ice cream shops or bakeries that dot the circle.

UTC Mall

For a more traditional shopping experience, the UTC Mall (University Town Center) is your go-to destination. Conveniently located just off I-75, it's easily accessible from all parts of Sarasota and the surrounding areas. As you approach the mall, you'll be greeted by a sleek and modern façade.

The UTC Mall offers a vast selection of retailers, from high-end department stores to popular national and international brands. Whether you're looking for designer fashion, accessories, electronics, or home goods, this shopping mecca has it all. With its airy, upscale atmosphere, the UTC Mall provides a comfortable and enjoyable shopping experience.

In addition to its extensive retail options, the UTC Mall is notable for its excellent dining choices. A variety of restaurants and cafes line the perimeter of the mall, offering a respite for shoppers to refuel and recharge. From casual eateries to upscale establishments showcasing diverse cuisines, there is something to please every palate.

Make the most of your shopping experience at UTC Mall by checking for any exclusive sales, special events, or promotions happening during your visit. The mall often hosts fashion shows, product launches, and community events, providing added excitement during your shopping excursion.

Downtown Sarasota

Downtown Sarasota serves as the bustling heart of the city, offering a blend of trendy boutiques, art galleries, and delicious dining options. Conveniently located near the coast, you can easily access downtown Sarasota by heading south on US-301 from the Sarasota-Bradenton International Airport.

As you step foot into downtown Sarasota, you'll be greeted by tree-lined streets, charming storefronts, and a welcoming atmosphere. The shopping experience here is all about variety and uniqueness. You'll find a mix of local businesses and well-known brands, making it an ideal place to discover one-of-a-kind souvenirs and fashionable pieces.

Begin your shopping adventure on Main Street, where designer boutiques and art galleries await. From trendy clothing stores to one-of-a-kind jewelry shops, you'll find an abundance of options to elevate your style. Explore Pineapple Avenue, a charming side street filled with upscale home decor stores, antique shops, and art galleries showcasing local talent.

One of the highlights of downtown Sarasota is the Sarasota Farmers Market, held every Saturday morning. Here, you can immerse yourself in the vibrant local scene, sample fresh produce, and peruse stalls filled with handmade crafts, local artwork, and delectable treats.

Westfield Sarasota Square

For a more traditional shopping experience, look no further than Westfield Sarasota Square. Situated just south of downtown Sarasota along US-41, this bustling mall is easily accessible from all parts of the city and surrounding areas.

Westfield Sarasota Square boasts a wide range of retailers, including popular department stores, national chains, and specialty shops. From fashion-forward clothing brands to technology outlets and home decor stores, you'll find everything you need in one convenient location.

Besides its extensive retail options, Westfield Sarasota Square offers a variety of dining choices. Grab a quick bite at the food court or savor a sit-down meal at one of the mall's restaurants. With its family-friendly atmosphere and inviting spaces, the mall provides an enjoyable shopping experience for everyone.

Gulf Gate Village

For a more unique and local shopping experience, head to Gulf Gate Village. Situated just south of downtown Sarasota along Gulf Gate Drive, this charming neighborhood shopping district has a laid-back ambiance.

Gulf Gate Village is known for its eclectic mix of shops, boutiques, and specialty stores. Here, you'll find everything from vintage clothing and antiques to handcrafted goods and artisanal products. Discover hidden gems as you explore the quaint streets lined with independent businesses and friendly local shop owners.

In addition to its shopping offerings, Gulf Gate Village is home to a variety of restaurants, cafes, and bars. Treat yourself to a delicious meal at a local eatery or unwind with a craft beer from a cozy taproom. With its relaxed, community-oriented atmosphere, Gulf Gate Village is the perfect place to explore and support local businesses.

As you wander through the shopping districts of downtown Sarasota, Westfield Sarasota Square, and Gulf Gate Village, keep an eye out for unique events and happenings. From art walks and street festivals to live music performances and community gatherings, Sarasota's shopping districts often host activities that add an extra touch of excitement to your shopping experience.

No matter which shopping district you choose to explore, Sarasota offers a myriad of options to satisfy your shopping desires. From trendy fashion finds to eclectic treasures, you're sure to discover something special to remind you of your memorable Sarasota vacation.

Local Products and Artisanal Crafts

Handcrafted Jewelry from Siesta Key

If you're looking to add a touch of elegance to your jewelry collection or find a special gift for someone, look no further than the handcrafted jewelry from Siesta Key. Siesta Key, known for its stunning beaches and artistic community, is home to many talented jewelry artisans who create beautiful pieces inspired by the tranquility of the island.

As you browse the jewelry shops along Siesta Key's main village area, you'll be mesmerized by the stunning array of options. From delicate necklaces adorned with seashells and gemstones to intricately designed bracelets and earrings, each piece reflects the coastal beauty of the area.

One of the popular materials used in the creation of Siesta Key's handcrafted jewelry is sterling silver, often paired with vibrant gemstones in various colors. Many artisans also incorporate elements of nature, such as seagrass or pieces of coral, into their designs, resulting in truly unique and eye-catching pieces.

When purchasing handcrafted jewelry from Siesta Key, not only are you acquiring a beautiful accessory, but you're also supporting local artisans and the rich artistic community of the area. The beauty and craftsmanship of these pieces serve as lasting reminders of your time spent in Sarasota's paradise.

Sarasota Honey

Another local product that you must add to your shopping list is Sarasota honey. Known for its high quality and distinct flavors, Sarasota honey is a true testament to the region's flourishing beekeeping industry and abundant natural resources.

Sarasota's diverse natural surroundings, including citrus groves, wildflowers, and palmetto patches, provide an ideal environment for bees to thrive and produce exceptional honey. As you explore Sarasota's farmer's markets or specialized honey stores, you'll find a wide range of honey varieties, each with its unique characteristics and flavors.

From the delicate sweetness of orange blossom honey to the robust and earthy notes of wildflower honey, Sarasota honey offers a taste of the region's natural bounty. You'll also find specialty varieties like tupelo honey, which has a smooth, buttery sweetness, and saw palmetto honey, known for its rich, caramel-like flavor.

Aside from its delightful taste, Sarasota honey also offers numerous health benefits. Raw, unfiltered honey is known for its antioxidant properties and potential allergy relief due to the trace amounts of pollen it contains. Choose locally sourced honey, as it may provide relief from pollen allergies specific to the region.

When purchasing Sarasota honey, consider buying from local beekeepers who prioritize sustainable and ethical beekeeping practices. This ensures that you're not only receiving a high-quality product but also supporting a vital industry that plays a significant role in Sarasota's ecosystem.

Artwork from Art Center Sarasota

Art Center Sarasota is a cultural haven that showcases the incredible talent of Sarasota's artistic community. As you stroll through the center, you'll be inspired by the wide array of artistic expressions on display. From breathtaking paintings to intricate sculptures and thought-provoking mixed-media pieces, each artwork tells a story and offers a glimpse into the creative minds of Sarasota's artists.

The Art Center regularly hosts rotating exhibitions, ensuring that there's always something new and exciting to discover. This dynamic approach allows you to experience fresh perspectives and artistic styles during each visit. As you wander through the gallery, take your time to appreciate the intricate brushstrokes, the attention to detail, and the emotions that radiate from each piece.

Sarasota-made Soap and Skincare Products

When it comes to self-care and pampering, Sarasota offers an abundance of locally made soap and skincare products that cater to even the most discerning tastes. These artisanal products are meticulously handcrafted by skilled artisans who infuse their creations with a deep understanding of natural ingredients and their beneficial properties.

From beautifully scented soaps to luxurious lotions and balms, Sarasota-made skincare products are designed to enhance your well-being and rejuvenate your body and soul. Indulge in the silky textures and enchanting fragrances that result from a careful blend of organic botanicals, nourishing oils, and plant-based essences.

Locally Roasted Coffee

Sarasota's coffee culture is an absolute delight for coffee enthusiasts. The city is home to a thriving coffee scene, with specialty shops and cafes that take great pride in sourcing high-quality beans from around the globe and roasting them to perfection.

When you enter one of these establishments, you'll be greeted by the rich aromas and the sound of beans being meticulously ground. Engage with knowledgeable baristas who are passionate about their craft, and let them guide you through the world of coffee flavors and brewing methods.

Local coffee roasters in Sarasota are known for their attention to detail and dedication to bringing out the unique characteristics of each bean. From light and floral roasts to bold and robust flavors, there is a world of taste to explore. Take your time to savor each sip, immersing yourself in the rich flavors that unfold.

Tips for Bargaining and Smart Shopping

When it comes to shopping and finding the perfect souvenirs in Sarasota, it is important to be equipped with some savvy techniques to enhance your experience and ensure you get the best value for your money. In this chapter, I will provide valuable tips and insights on bargaining and smart shopping, allowing you to enjoy your Sarasota shopping adventure.

Research Prices and Compare

Before stepping foot into any shop or market, take the time to research the average prices for the items you're interested in. This will give you a strong stand to negotiate. Seek out multiple sources, such as online listings, local guides, or fellow traveler recommendations to have the typical price range. With this knowledge, you'll be better prepared to recognize good deals and avoid overpaying.

Additionally, make it a practice to compare prices between different vendors. Sarasota offers a diverse shopping landscape, with various stores and markets catering to different needs and budgets. By visiting multiple locations and comparing prices, you can ensure that you're getting the best possible value for your desired items.

Develop Your Bargaining Skills

Bargaining is a common practice in many markets and stores in Sarasota. It can be an exciting and rewarding experience, allowing you to secure great deals and interact with local vendors. To excel in bargaining, consider the following tips:

- Be Confident and Polite: Approach negotiations with a friendly and respectful attitude. Engage in pleasant conversation with the vendor before discussing prices, showcasing your genuine interest in their products.
- Start Low, But Reasonable: When making an initial offer, go slightly below your desired price, but ensure it remains reasonable. This provides room for negotiation without disrespecting the vendor's craft or goods.
- Show Commitment: Express your interest in purchasing the item while highlighting any similar alternatives you've seen in other shops. This indicates your willingness to explore other options, motivating the vendor to offer a better deal.
- Bundle Items: If you're interested in multiple items from the same vendor, consider bundling them together. Vendors are often more inclined to offer a discounted price when they can make a larger sale.

145

- Walk Away if Needed: Sometimes, vendors may not budge on their price. As difficult as it may be, don't be afraid to politely walk away. This can create a sense of urgency and often prompts the vendor to reconsider their offer.

Timing and Seasonality

Consider the timing of your shopping excursion in Sarasota. Like many destinations, certain times of the year may offer better deals and discounts. The off-peak tourist season or times when there are local festivals or events could be opportune moments to find great bargains.

Additionally, keep seasonality in mind when shopping for specific items. Some products, like swimwear or holiday decorations, may have significant price reductions during the off-season. Take advantage of these opportunities to save money and acquire higher-quality items at lower costs.

Authenticity and Quality

When shopping for souvenirs, it's important to prioritize authenticity and quality. Sarasota offers a range of unique handmade products, locally sourced goods, and artistic creations. To ensure you're purchasing genuine items, consider the following:

- Research Local Craftsmanship: Familiarize yourself with the traditional crafts and artisanal products of Sarasota. This will help you recognize and appreciate authentic pieces.
- Seek Recommendations: Ask locals, hotel staff, or other trusted sources for recommendations on reputable shops and markets that showcase authentic and high-quality products.
- Examine the Details: Inspect items carefully before purchasing. Look for indicators of craftsmanship, such as intricate detailing, quality materials, and finishing touches that demonstrate the product's authenticity and durability.
- Support Local Artisans: Seek out items made by local artisans and small businesses. Not only will this ensure the uniqueness of your souvenirs, but it will also support the local community and foster the preservation of traditional craftsmanship.

By paying attention to authenticity and quality, you'll not only bring home souvenirs that truly represent the spirit of Sarasota but also contribute to the sustainability of local industries.

Stay Open-Minded and Enjoy the Experience

Finally, while it's important to be well-informed and prepared, don't forget to enjoy the experience of shopping in Sarasota. The process of exploring different shops, engaging with vendors, and discovering unique treasures is part of the charm of any destination.

Embrace the vibrant atmosphere, immerse yourself in the local culture, and savor the moments spent browsing through markets and shops. Strike up conversations, learn the stories behind the products, and appreciate the artistry and craftsmanship that go into each item you encounter.

Thus, incorporating these tips into your Sarasota shopping experience will empower you to become a smart shopper and a skilled negotiator.

Chapter 9: Travel Itinerary

When planning a trip to Sarasota, Florida, it's essential to have a well-crafted itinerary to make the most of your time in this beautiful city. Whether you have three, seven, or even fourteen days to spare, I've got you covered. Here, I will present detailed itineraries, including a 3-day, 7-day, and 14-day option, and offer the flexibility to customize your itinerary based on your preferences. Let's delve into the possibilities that await you in Sarasota.

3-Day Itinerary

If you find yourself with a short but exciting three-day visit to Sarasota, this itinerary will ensure you get a taste of the city's highlights, blending its cultural heritage, natural beauty, and iconic attractions.

Day 1: Immerse Yourself in Culture

Start your first day by exploring the vibrant cultural scene in Sarasota.

Morning

Begin with a visit to The Ringling, a prominent museum complex. Delve into the world of art as you marvel at the impressive collection featuring artists like Rubens and Velázquez. Explore the beautifully manicured gardens and be awestruck by the Ca' d'Zan mansion's magnificent architecture.

Afternoon

Head downtown to Main Street, where you'll find an array of charming boutiques, art galleries, and delightful cafés. Take your time exploring the local shops and enjoy a leisurely lunch at one of the farm-to-table eateries.

Afterward, indulge your creative side by visiting the Arts District. Explore the galleries and studios, where talented local artists showcase their masterpieces. You might even find the perfect artwork to take home as a memento.

Evening

Savor a delectable seafood dinner at one of the waterfront restaurants in St. Armands Circle. Afterward, take a stroll along Lido Beach and witness the captivating sunset over the Gulf of Mexico—a truly magical experience.

Day 2: Beaches and Wildlife

Dedicate your second day in Sarasota to exploring the pristine beaches and encountering the local wildlife.

Morning

Start by visiting Siesta Key Beach, renowned for its powder-soft white sand and crystal-clear waters. Take a refreshing dip or relax under the shade of an umbrella, absorbing the serene surroundings.

Afternoon

Enjoy a picnic lunch at Turtle Beach while immersing yourself in the breathtaking coastal views. For a unique adventure, embark on an eco-tour through the nearby mangrove tunnels, where you'll witness fascinating wildlife and learn about the delicate ecosystem.

Evening

Spend the evening at the Marie Selby Botanical Gardens, a tropical oasis featuring stunning flora. Take a stroll through the gardens, letting the fragrant blooms and serene ambiance transport you to another world. If available, consider attending one of the special evening events or installations for an enchanting experience.

Day 3: Nature and Wildlife Encounters

Explore the natural wonders of Sarasota on your final day.

Morning

Head out to Myakka River State Park for an exciting morning adventure. Take an exhilarating airboat tour through the expansive wetlands, keeping an eye out for alligators, birds, and other fascinating wildlife. Alternatively, explore the park's hiking trails, where you can immerse yourself in the diverse flora and fauna.

Afternoon

Savor a picnic lunch surrounded by the park's picturesque scenery, soaking up the serenity of nature. In the afternoon, visit the Mote Marine Laboratory & Aquarium, where you can learn about marine conservation and interact with captivating sea life.

Evening

Conclude your three-day itinerary with an elegant dinner at a downtown restaurant. As the day draws to a close, explore Sarasota's vibrant nightlife by catching a live performance at one of the city's renowned theaters or enjoying a relaxing drink at a trendy bar.

7-Day Itinerary

If you have a week to spare in Sarasota, you can delve even deeper into the city's offerings. This extended itinerary allows you to explore more attractions and indulge in various outdoor activities:

Days 1-3: Follow the suggestions provided in the 3-day itinerary.

Day 4: Cultural Delights and Waterfront Charm

Morning

Spend your fourth day visiting the Asolo Repertory Theatre, renowned for its exceptional performances and innovative productions. Immerse yourself in the world of theater and witness the incredible talent on display.

Afternoon

Enjoy a leisurely lunch at a downtown eatery, sampling the diverse culinary options available. Then, take a scenic cruise on Sarasota Bay, savoring the spectacular views of the city's skyline and waterfront.

Evening

Explore the vibrant dining scene of Downtown Sarasota, where you can find a variety of restaurants offering international cuisines. After dinner, take a stroll along the picturesque Bayfront Park, enjoying the cool evening breeze and taking in the beautiful waterfront ambiance.

Day 5: Nature and Art

Morning

Embark on an adventure to the Celery Fields, a wildlife oasis teeming with birds, reptiles, and native plants. Take a walk along the boardwalks and enjoy birdwatching, capturing stunning photographs of the diverse bird species that call this area home.

Afternoon

Visit the Sarasota Jungle Gardens for a unique experience in nature. Explore the lush gardens filled with exotic vegetation and encounter colorful parrots, playful primates, and reptiles of all shapes and sizes.

Evening

Head to the vibrant Towles Court Artist Colony, where you can immerse yourself in the local art scene. Explore the galleries and studios, interact with artists, and admire their captivating works. End the evening with a delightful dinner at one of the nearby restaurants, which offers a blend of international cuisines.

Days 6-7: Beach Paradise and Island Exploration

Morning

Spend these two days exploring the nearby islands and their stunning beaches. Start with a visit to Longboat Key for a relaxing morning on its pristine shores, enjoying water activities such as swimming, paddleboarding, or simply lounging under the sun.

Afternoon

Head over to Anna Maria Island, where you can grab lunch at a beachfront restaurant overlooking the azure waters. Continue your island adventure by exploring the island's charming shops and boutiques, and don't forget to indulge in some delicious ice cream.

Evening

Witness one of Sarasota's most breathtaking natural phenomena by visiting Siesta Key Beach for a sunset drum circle. Join in the rhythmic beats and celebratory atmosphere as the sun dips below the horizon, turning the sky into a vibrant canvas.

14-Day Itinerary

If you have two weeks to dedicate to your Sarasota exploration, you have the opportunity to fully immerse yourself in the city's multifaceted charm. This itinerary combines the highlights of the previous itineraries with additional experiences to discover:

Days 1-7: Follow the suggestions provided in the 7-Day Itinerary.

Days 8-14: Adventure and Eclectic Experiences

Days 8-10

Venture beyond Sarasota and explore the nearby Everglades National Park. Embark on exhilarating airboat tours, go kayaking through mangrove tunnels, and observe the unique wildlife that thrives in this diverse ecosystem.

Days 11-12

Discover Sarasota's vibrant arts and theater scene by attending performances at the Sarasota Opera House and the Westcoast Black Theatre Troupe. Additionally, visit the various art galleries and museums in the city to enrich your cultural experience.

Days 13-14

Indulge in a luxury spa day, allowing yourself to unwind and rejuvenate. Sarasota offers an array of top-notch spas where you can pamper yourself with massages, facials, and other relaxing treatments. Finish off your trip with a farewell dinner at one of the city's renowned fine dining establishments, savoring the culinary masterpieces created by talented chefs.

Customized Itinerary

If none of the suggested itineraries match your preferences or if you prefer a mix of experiences, I offer you the option to create your own customized itinerary. Decide which attractions, activities, and locations appeal to you the most and create a schedule that suits your interests and desired pace.

Remember to incorporate Sarasota's cultural offerings, natural beauty, culinary delights, and opportunities for outdoor adventures. Take advantage of the stunning beaches, visit the museums and galleries that catch your eye, and explore the local nature reserves and parks to appreciate the diverse flora and fauna of the region.

By personalizing your itinerary, you can create a truly unique and unforgettable experience in Sarasota, tailored to your tastes and preferences.

Chapter 10: Practical Information

As you embark on your journey to Sarasota, Florida, it's essential to equip yourself with practical information to ensure a safe, enjoyable, and sustainable travel experience. This chapter covers important aspects such as safety and health tips, sustainable travel practices, language and communication, and essential phrases.

Safety and Health Tips

Ensuring your safety and well-being during your visit to Sarasota is paramount. Here are few tips to keep in mind:

- Stay Hydrated: Sarasota's warm climate can lead to dehydration, especially during outdoor activities. Make sure to use a reusable water bottle and drink enough fluids throughout the day.
- Sun Protection: To shield yourself from the sun's harmful effects, wear sunscreen with a high SPF, along with sunglasses and a wide-brimmed hat. Find shade during the sun's peak hours, usually between 10:00am and 4:00 pm.
- Beach Safety: When swimming in the Gulf of Mexico, always adhere to lifeguard instructions and swim in designated areas. Watch out for rip currents and heed warning signs posted on the beach.
- Mosquito Prevention: Florida's subtropical climate makes it susceptible to mosquitoes, especially during the summer months. Use insect repellent containing DEET, wear long sleeves and pants, and avoid outdoor activities during dawn and dusk when mosquitoes are most active.
- Emergency Preparedness: Familiarize yourself with emergency procedures and contact information for local authorities, hospitals, and emergency services. Keep a copy of your travel documents and important phone numbers handy.

Sustainable Travel Practices

As a responsible traveler, it's essential to minimize your environmental impact and support sustainable tourism initiatives. Here are some ways you can practice sustainable travel in Sarasota:

- Reduce, Reuse, Recycle: Participate in recycling programs and minimize waste generation by using reusable water bottles, bags, and containers.
- Support Local Businesses: Opt for locally-owned accommodations, restaurants, and shops to support the local economy and community.
- Respect Wildlife and Natural Habitats: Observe wildlife from a safe distance and refrain from feeding or disturbing animals. Stay on designated trails.
- Use Sustainable Transportation: Explore Sarasota by walking, biking, or using public transportation whenever possible.

Language and Communication

While English is the predominant language spoken in Sarasota, you may encounter cultural and linguistic diversity in this vibrant city. Here are few language and communication tips:

- English is Widely Spoken: English is the primary language spoken in Sarasota, and you'll find that most locals are fluent in English.
- Multicultural Environment: Sarasota is home to a diverse population, including residents from various cultural backgrounds and nationalities.

Essential Phrases

While English is widely spoken in Sarasota, learning a few basic phrases can enhance your travel experience and foster positive interactions with locals.

Final Thoughts, Recommendations, and Conclusion

As you conclude your comprehensive exploration of Sarasota, Florida, through this guide, "Sarasota Travel Guide: Discover and Explore the Cultural Coast of Florida," it's clear that Sarasota offers a unique blend of cultural richness, architectural beauty, stunning natural landscapes, profound historical depth, and beauty beaches. This guide has endeavored to provide you with insightful and detailed accounts of what makes Sarasota not just a destination but a vibrant community full of life and artistry.

Reflecting on Sarasota's Unique Offerings

Sarasota is a treasure trove If you seek more than just a holiday; it offers an experience steeped in cultural engagement and leisurely pursuits. The city is renowned not only for its pristine beaches, such as the world-famous Siesta Key Beach, but also for its robust cultural scene encompassing live performances, museums, and galleries. The architectural splendor of the area—from the John and Mable Ringling Museum of Art to the modern designs scattered throughout the city—adds a layer of aesthetic pleasure to the visit.

Recommendations for You

To maximize your visit to Sarasota, consider the following suggestions:

- Time Your Visit: Align your trip with key cultural events or festivals to experience Sarasota at its most vibrant. The Sarasota Film Festival and the Sarasota Music Festival are prime examples where the city's artistic spirit is especially palpable.
- Explore Beyond the Beaches: While Sarasota's beaches are enticing, its cultural institutions like the Sarasota Ballet, the Opera, and numerous theaters offer enriching experiences that showcase the city's commitment to the arts.

- Engage with Local Culture: Visit local markets, dine at farm-to-table restaurants, and explore the city's historical sites to gain a deeper understanding of Sarasota's heritage and community life.

Travel Tips

- Accommodation: Book well in advance if planning to visit during peak tourist seasons or around major events.
- Transportation: Renting a car is advisable for convenient travel around the city and to nearby attractions. However, public transportation and biking are excellent in downtown areas.
- Weather Preparedness: Florida's weather can be unpredictable. Pack accordingly, and always check the weather forecast ahead of your visit.

Engaging with the Community

One of the joys of traveling is the opportunity to immerse oneself in the local community, and Sarasota's welcoming atmosphere makes this particularly rewarding. Participating in community events, supporting local businesses, and interacting with residents can enrich your travel experience and provide insights not typically accessible through standard tourist paths.

Sustainability Practices

As a visitor, maintaining mindfulness about environmental impact is crucial. Sarasota prides itself on its natural beauty, and contributing to the preservation of these natural resources ensures their longevity for future visitors. Practices such as respecting wildlife, using eco-friendly sunscreens, and participating in local conservation efforts can make a significant difference.

Conclusion

Sarasota, Florida, is a destination where every visit can be as dynamic and enriching as one desires. From its sandy shores to its artistic corners, the city offers a myriad of activities and experiences that cater to all interests and ages. This guide hopes to have provided you with the necessary tools and knowledge to ensure that your time in Sarasota is not just memorable but also meaningful. Whether you seek relaxation, cultural enrichment, or adventurous exploration, Sarasota promises a wealth of experiences waiting to be discovered. Enjoy your journey in this splendid city, where every path and every sunset tell a story.

Sarasota, Florida Travel Planner

Sarasota

Date:_____

Town:_____

Travel Planner

Monday	Tuesday	Wednesday

Thursday	Friday	Saturday

Checklist	Note

Sarasota

Travel Planner

Monday	Tuesday	Wednesday

Thursday	Friday	Saturday

Checklist	Note

Sarasota

Travel Planner

Monday	Tuesday	Wednesday

Thursday	Friday	Saturday

Checklist	Note

Sarasota

Travel Planner

| Date: _____ |
| Town: _____ |

Monday	Tuesday	Wednesday

Thursday	Friday	Saturday

Checklist	Note

Sarasota, Florida Itinerary

Name:	Duration of Stay:

Hotel Name:	
Arrival Date:	Flight No:

Days	What To Do	Budget
01		
02		
03		
04		
Note		

Name:		Duration of Stay:
Hotel Name:		
Arrival Date:		Flight No:

Days	What To Do	Budget
01		
02		
03		
04		
Note		

164

Name:	Duration of Stay:
Hotel Name:	
	Flight No:
Arrival Date:	

Days	What To Do	Budget
01		
02		
03		
04		
Note		

Name:		Duration of Stay:
Hotel Name:		
Arrival Date:		Flight No:

Days	What To Do	Budget
01		
02		
03		
04		
Note		

Printed in Great Britain
by Amazon

58991774R00096